POETRY FROM CRESCENT MOON

William Shakespeare: *Selected Sonnets and Verse*
edited, with an introduction by Mark Tuley

William Shakespeare: *The Sonnets*
edited and introduced by Mark Tuley

*Shakespeare: Love, Poetry and Magic
in Shakespeare's Sonnets and Plays*
by B.D. Barnacle

Edmund Spenser: *Heavenly Love: Selected Poems*
selected and introduced by Teresa Page

Robert Herrick: *Delight In Disorder: Selected Poems*
edited and introduced by M.K. Pace

Sir Thomas Wyatt: *Love For Love: Selected Poems*
selected and introduced by Louise Cooper

John Donne: *Air and Angels: Selected Poems*
selected and introduced by A.H. Ninham

D.H. Lawrence: *Being Alive: Selected Poems*
edited with an introduction by Margaret Elvy

D.H. Lawrence: Symbolic Landscapes
by Jane Foster

D.H. Lawrence: Infinite Sensual Violence
by M.K. Pace

Percy Bysshe Shelley: *Paradise of Golden Lights: Selected Poems*
selected and introduced by Charlotte Greene

Thomas Hardy: *Her Haunting Ground: Selected Poems*
edited, with an introduction by A.H. Ninham

Sexing Hardy: Thomas Hardy and Feminism
by Margaret Elvy

Emily Brontë: *Darkness and Glory: Selected Poems*
selected and introduced by Miriam Chalk

John Keats: *Bright Star: Selected Poems*
edited with an introduction by Miriam Chalk

Henry Vaughan: *A Great Ring of Pure and Endless Light: Selected Poems*
selected and introduced by A.H. Ninham

The Crescent Moon Book of Love Poetry
edited by Louise Cooper

The Crescent Moon Book of Mystical Poetry in English
edited by Carol Appleby

The Crescent Moon Book of Nature Poetry From Langland to Lawrence
edited by Margaret Elvy

The Crescent Moon Book of Metaphysical Poetry
edited and introduced by Charlotte Greene

The Crescent Moon Book of Elizabethan Love Poetry
edited and introduced by Carol Appleby

The Crescent Moon Book of Romantic Poetry
edited and introduced by L.M. Poole

Blinded By Her Light The Love-Poetry of Robert Graves
by Jeremy Mark Robinson

The Best of Peter Redgrove's Poetry: The Book of Wonders
by Peter Redgrove, edited and introduced by Jeremy Mark Robinson

Peter Redgrove: Here Comes the Flood
by Jeremy Mark Robinson

Sex-Magic-Poetry-Cornwall: A Flood of Poems
by Peter Redgrove, edited with an essay by Jeremy Mark Robinson

Brigitte's Blue Heart
by Jeremy Reed

Claudia Schiffer's Red Shoes
by Jeremy Reed

By-Blows: Uncollected Poems
by D.J. Enright

Petrarch, Dante and the Troubadours: The Religion of Love and Poetry
by Cassidy Hughes

Arthur Rimbaud: *Selected Poems*
edited and translated by Andrew Jary

Arthur Rimbaud: *A Season in Hell*
edited and translated by Andrew Jary

Rimbaud: Arthur Rimbaud and the Magic of Poetry
by Jeremy Mark Robinson

Friedrich Hölderlin: *Hölderlin's Songs of Light: Selected Poems*
translated by Michael Hamburger

Rainer Maria Rilke: *Dance the Orange:* Selected Poems
translated by Michael Hamburger

Rilke: Space, Essence and Angels in the Poetry of Rainer Maria Rilke
by B.D. Barnacle

German Romantic Poetry: Goethe, Novalis,
Heine, Hölderlin, Schlegel, Schiller
by Carol Appleby

Arseny Tarkovsky: *Life, Life: Selected Poems*
translated by Virginia Rounding

Emily Dickinson: *Wild Nights: Selected Poems*
selected and introduced by Miriam Chalk

Cavafy: Anatomy of a Soul
by Matt Crispin

Jeremy Robinson has written many critical studies, including *Hayao Miyazaki*, *Walerian Borowczyk*, *Arthur Rimbaud*, and *The Sacred Cinema of Andrei Tarkovsky*, plus literary monographs on: Shakespeare; Samuel Beckett; Thomas Hardy; André Gide; Robert Graves; and John Cowper Powys.

It's amazing for me to see my work treated with such passion and respect. There is nothing resembling it in the U.S. in relation to my work.

Andrea Dworkin (on *Andrea Dworkin*)

This model monograph – it is an exemplary job, and I'm very proud that he has accorded me a couple of mentions... The subject matter of his book is beautifully organised and dead on beam.

Lawrence Durrell (on *The Light Eternal: A Study of J.M.W. Turner*)

His poetry is very good deep moving stuff.

Cloud Nine magazine

Jeremy Robinson's poetry is certainly jammed with ideas, and I find it very interesting for that reason. It's certainly a strong imprint of his personality.

Colin Wilson

Sex-Magic-Poetry-Cornwall is a very rich essay... It is a very good piece... vastly stimulating and insightful.

Peter Redgrove

Peter Redgrove
Here Comes the Flood

Peter Redgrove
Here Comes the Flood
A Study of His Poetry

Jeremy Mark Robinson

CRESCENT MOON

CRESCENT MOON PUBLISHING
P.O. Box 393
Maidstone
Kent, ME14 5XU
United Kingdom

First published 1994. Third edition 2011.
© Jeremy Robinson 1994, 2011.
Poems © Peter Redgrove 1994, 2011.

Printed and bound in the U.S.A.
Set in Book Antiqua 10 on 14pt.
Designed by Radiance Graphics.

The right of Jeremy Mark Robinson to be identified as the author of this book has been asserted generally in accordance with sections 77 and 78 of the Copyright, Designs and Patents Act 1988.

All rights reserved. No part of this book may be reprinted or reproduced, stored in a retrieval system, or transmitted, in any form or by any means, electronic, mechanical, photocopying, recording or otherwise, without permission from the publisher.

British Library Cataloguing in Publication data

Robinson, Jeremy Mark
Peter Redgrove: Here Comes the Flood: A Study of His Poetry
1. Redgrove, Peter – Criticism and Interpretation
I. Title
821.914

ISBN-13 9781861712943

Contents

        Acknowledgements   11
        Abbreviations   13
        Preface For the 3rd Edition   21
        Preface For the New Edition   23

One   *The Outer and Inner Life*   27
Two   *Alchemy of the Word : Redgrove's Poetics*   53
        Illustrations   95
Three   *Adventures in the Mother-World :*
        Extra-Sensuous Perception   103
Four   *Feminism and the Goddess*   157
Five   *Sex Magic, Sex Alchemy, Sex Yoga*   179
Six   *Critical Appraisal*   193

        Bibliography   201

Acknowledgements

Thanks to Peter Redgrove, and to Geraldine Snowball, Karen Arthurs, Cassidy Hughes, Tony Maestri and Cindy Robinson

Abbreviations

SS	"Scientist of the Strange", interview
Laz	"Lazarus and the Visionary Truth", interview
NCW	*The Nature of Cold Weather and Other Poems*
WM	*At the White Monument*
For	*The Force*
Dr	*Dr Faust's Sea-Spiral Spirit*
ICS	*In the Country of the Skin*
Ark	*From Every Chink of the Ark*
WNP	*The Weddings at Nether Powers*
AB	*The Apple-Broadcast*
WW	*The Working of Water*
Man	*The Man Named East*
Mud	*The Mudlark Poems*
IHS	*In the Hall of the Saurians*
Sel	*Poems 1954-1987*
FE	*The First Earthquake*
Tar	*Dressed As For a Tarot Pack*
UR	*Under the Reservoir,*
Lab	*The Laborators*
Ab	*Abyssophone*
OE	*Orchard End*
FVC	*From the Virgil Caverns*
BG	*The Black Goddess and the Sixth Sense*
AFW	*Alchemy For Women*
CIT	*A Crystal of Industrial Time*
AJ	*An Alchemical Journal*

Bees At Land's-End

Music comes, a giant's hum from below the sea-line,
Clanging of cliffs rocked with a salty hiss
Leaping out from the crack of a rounded stone
Where light pours crystalline, in liquid granite,
Bouncing onto blue sea-washed calcite.

An aeroplane murmurs above, banking
For Sennen Cove and Land's End aerodrome.
The sound comes deeper now, but it's not
The arcade screech of a million fruit machines
That make Penzance glitter like Las Vegas.

It's not the whine of pylons in a high wind,
Or the limpid song of a star-bound lark.
No, the sound's in the belly, in the plexus,
It's boulders rolling on the sea bed, heard
In the out-lying tunnel of a mine.

Falling in crashes, the waves rock our bodies,
Billowed out, wet, full as a galleon's sail,
And drenched in the blood of fantasy pirates,
We voyagers on the high seas of the soul,
Treasure chests spilled open on booming canvas.

Sea on all sides, like being in a mirror,
The blue-on-blue of sea and sky, sea and sky,
With the sun sewn under our skin in a pouch
Which expands and illuminates the body
So all's warmth and again the taste of salt.

The whisper now of pampas grass and strange plants,
The twin paths that snake below the steep slopes,
The gulleys open up sudden and vicious,
You could fall, knowing nothing for seconds,
Then… the impact with rock or water - nirvana.

Still the sound swells, as you enter the farm.
Goats with pink eyes, wood, straw, cream teas, chickens,
And a marvellous glass honey bee hive,
The bees at work in the honeycomb city,
The Queen Bee marked by a white spot on her back.

Here's where the music rises, this bee hive,
The sound rolls out over all of Cornwall,
The choiring of celestial angels, the bees,
They're so small, yet so loud, antenna tuned in
To the global broadcast of the ocean.

Jeremy Mark Robinson

Written after visiting Peter Redgrove in Cornwall, 1993.

Everything can become magical-work.

Novalis (*Pollen*)

Peter Redgrove

Preface

This book is an expanded and rewritten version of the book *Sex-Magic-Poetry-Cornwall: A Flood of Poems* by Peter Redgrove (1932-2003). I wrote the essay that accompanied the selection of Redgrove's poems. The book was first published by Crescent Moon in 1994.

This book discusses many of Redgrove's best poems, some of which are printed in full. I have drawn on all of Redgrove's poetry from his very first books to the latest work, including unpublished poems. Where possible, I have cited references to the Penguin edition of his selected poems, *Poems 1954-1987*, the best introduction to his poetic career. The book *The Cyclopean Mistress* (Bloodaxe, 1993) usefully gathers together some of Redgrove's prose poems. These two books are cited throughout this book, although Redgrove's later poetry, written since the 1987 *Poems* is his richest to date, so I have included discussions of poems drawn from *The First Earthquake* (1989), *Dressed As For a Tarot Pack* (1990), *Under the Reservoir* (1992), *The Laborators* (1993), *My Father's Trapdoors* (1994) and *Abyssophone* (1995). There are further Redgrove books published since the first edition of this book in 1994, such as *Orchard's End, Sheen* and *A Speaker For the Silver*

Goddess; these poetry books have been discussed in the companion editions of *Sex-Magic-Poetry-Cornwall* and *The Best of Peter Redgrove's Poetry* (both 2007). I have quoted from Redgrove's letters, which are identified by date. I have concentrated on Redgrove's poetry, rather than his fiction and articles, because he regards his poetry as central to his work.

No study of Peter Redgrove is complete with many references to his second wife, Penelope Shuttle. She is crucially important in his work and life. Their poetry merges at many points, as with other artists who work and live together. Redgrove's poems are not 'co-authored' in the usual sense: Redgrove writes them. But the Shuttle-Redgrove partnership needs to be kept in mind when reading Redgrove's poems.

I would like to thank Peter Redgrove.

Jeremy Mark Robinson
Kent, England, 1994

Preface For the New Edition

For this edition of *Peter Redgrove: Here Comes the Flood*, we cannot print whole poems by Peter Redgrove (due to the people who control Redgrove's estate).

This is a pity, partly because Redgrove had been delighted by the approach I had taken to his work. We corresponded often about this book and the two companion books. Here is a selection of Redgrove's letters to me:

Thanks very much for your exciting draft. I'm of course very glad that you feel the poems sustain and feed back the vision you describe... Some of your phrases were personally helpful to me... What you write becomes a great rush of invocation and suggestion – as I say, I'm glad that the poems stand up in the force of your (ever welcome) enthusiasm... It is very good for me that the *Alchemical Journal* works as it does on you – there is that shock of recognition which the imagination is prone to languish...

This is a very rich essay you have written... I greatly look forward to seeing it in its final form – it is very energising for me to have your response to this work – poems that I thought had closed are opening again! ...I hope I have written enough to show

how appreciate I am of your voracious reading and your response.

Peter Redgrove, April 14, 1993

Your essay has an infectious enthusiasm, which I'm grateful for, and I especially like the places where you actually grapple with the language of my poems, which is like writing them again. It is a very good piece, which carries the reader with it... Your own approach is irreplaceable because it seems to us founded on your own individuality and personal experience of my poems – which is vastly gratifying... in the majority it is vastly stimulating and insightful. Always, I am grateful to you for your trouble, and your deep response to what I have written.

Peter Redgrove, letter, May 19, 1993

Very many thanks for 'Our Book' which I shall always treasure. It is like a brightly-lighted box in which you have turned on all the light of your enthusiasm, so that the poems glow like the calcite of the underground rocks do in the ultra-violet of the poem in the Esplumeor sequence... This is spooky for me since the poems have resurrected themselves – there is usually so little feedback that one cannot believe one has written something that one knew one was writing them, until the circuit is closed again and the current flows... It was a good idea of yours to use the image of the waterfall beating on the head of the poet or the reader... There is a right emphasis on ecstasy – that is indeed the point.

I don't think anybody has said this before, I think you have chosen the poems well, and written well about them. Thank you! I shall always be grateful... It is wonderful to see the poems responding to your insights. Penelope [Shuttle] says that your readings of the individual texts in your essay are among the best she has seen anywhere.

I like very much the way you have resurrected poems I had forgotten worked, like the clothes magic-wet and the alchemical honeymoon – I thought they didn't work because nobody had put them in context before of the elemental life that nudges into them always – and I like the cragginess of the prose poems in contrast. Your choice of quotations is excellent throughout, and this is the real point – plus enthusiasm… it is like a laser gas into which you pump your enthusiastic energy, there is a sudden shift of atomic orbits, and the texts shine with their own weird and natural light!

Peter Redgrove, letter, November 7, 1993

Peter Redgrove was a wonderful collaborator, exchanging so many letters and ideas, sending me many books, pamphlets and interviews, and explaining his themes, images and poems in detail.

Jeremy Mark Robinson
Kent, England, 2011

One

The Outer and Inner Life

There are few men of such range of personality, human learning and understanding and zest for life. He is the most prolific poet of the last twenty years and one of the most enigmatic. He writes of everything.

Martin Booth (227)

Life and Context

Peter Redgrove's life is well-documented elsewhere, in his many interviews.[1] Born in Kingston-upon-Thames, Surrey, in 1932, he went from public school to Cambridge University to read natural sciences. Redgrove worked as a scientist, a copywriter, and also taught at Falmouth College of Art for years (as well as in Buffalo and Leeds). He married Barbara Sherlock, a sculptor, in 1954; they had two children. Redgrove's second wife was poet Penelope Shuttle (they had a daughter, Zoe). He spent much of his later life in Cornwall.

---

[1] see Martin Booth, 225f; Lucie-Smith, ed: *British Poetry Since 1945*, Penguin 1985; various handbooks and directories on contemporary writers, etc.

Peter Redgrove: Here Comes the Flood

Peter Redgrove was one of the Group poets, and is placed by critics in the Ted Hughes/ Sylvia Plath/ Philip Hobsbaum circle of poets. He speaks warmly of Ted Hughes, but says his poetry is quite different.[2] 'Hughes is certainly a marvellous poet' says Redgrove (SS). It is interesting to compare Hughes and Redgrove. 'If Hughes is Grünewald, Redgrove is Bosch' writes Jeff Nutall. They are very different poets. They both use similar formal aspects of poetry: free verse structures, very rarely rhymed, and the three line stanza that Sylvia Plath employed so powerfully (in her famous 'Lady Lazarus', for example). But the imagery, goals, allusions and outlook of Hughes and Redgrove are quite different. Hughes grew successful: his books are used in schools, lauded by critics, he wrote stage plays with the luminary of the theatrical world, Peter Brook, and eventually Hughes became Poet Laureate.

Peter Redgrove, however, no lesser a poet than Ted Hughes in any way, is still on the sidelines of the poetry establishment. He may be 'high priest of the orgasmic rites of the underworld', as Anne Stevenson dubbed him, and 'for long England's leading ecological poet *avant la lettre*', as Terry Eagleton wrote, but only for a select coterie of critics and readers. He is respected but still largely misunderstood. He does not write about grimy lives in grim Northern towns such as Huddersfield or Hull, as if the working class 'don't let the bastards get you down' sort of art was the only kind of poetic authenticity. His social commentary is oblique (but he does pinpoint one aspect of provincial Britain neatly in this sentence from *Dr Lucky*: '[o]ne can live in Agatha Christie country pretending that there is neither the atomic bomb nor Aids and not even except as an ancient whisper, Adolf Hitler.' (CM, 125) He seldom uses cultural signposts or allusions (to films, TV, radio, newspapers, commodities), and he is not 'political' in the party political/ classist/ media-based sense. But then, if

---
[2] see Redgrove on Hughes in interviews, "Lazarus and the Visionary Truth", "Scientist of the Strange", etc.

Peter Redgrove: Here Comes the Flood

Henry Vaughan wrote poems such as 'The Morning-Watch', 'The World', 'The Retreat' and 'The Night' today, he would be laughed at. It would be the same with Shelley in his breathless 'Prometheus Unbound', or Thomas Wyatt in his courtly, Petrarchan lyrics, or Hölderlin in his ecstatic Hellenic lyrics, or Spenser in his dream of Albion, *The Faerie Queene*. It's not simply that poets such as Keats, Sidney, Tasso, Scève, Traherne, Herbert and Clare speak in 'old-fashioned', heavily stylized forms, it's also that they speak of 'great' themes in a 'grand' manner. This form of poetry, of poetry as religious and visionary, is regarded suspiciously today. Redgrove's lack of popularity may be due in part to the antipathy of critics to religious, mythic, visionary and magical art. There are critics, for instance, who still insist that a myth is a 'lie'. This is really annoying, this continued misunderstanding of something as fundamental as mythology. Too many critics have not understood the basic sacrality and importance of mythopoeia. They have not read Mircea Eliade, Robert Briffault, Gerald Massey, C.G. Jung, Marija Gimbutas, Marie-Louise von Franz, Esther Harding, Karl Kerenyi, Julius Evola, Titus Burckhardt, Erich Neumann, John Rhys, William James, Freud, Heinrich Zimmer, William Thompson, Barbara Walker and Rudolf Otto, to name but a tiny number of recent writers. Speaking of *The Wise Wound*, Redgrove says 'I have blotted my copybook irretrievably red for danger by collaborating in a book on menstruation, and have received many insults from the masculinist establishment as a result.' (We, 140)

Peter Redgrove: Here Comes the Flood

Ted Hughes and Peter Redgrove

Unlike Peter Redgrove's poetic world, Ted Hughes's poetic world comes out of Shakespeare in *King Lear*. In particular the *Lear* of the heath scenes, with all that wind, rain, barren earth, darkness/light, craggy hills and the old king's tormented psyche toppling over into an inner void. Seamus Heaney likens Hughes to Poor Tom. Ted Hughes' poetic world is rather as if the Harlech 'green world' of early Robert Graves (circa 'Rocky Acres') had been re-shot by Ingmar Bergman at the height of his *The Virgin Spring* period. It is the paradisal world of childhood made existentially painful, acutely aware of the 'great themes' of poetry: birth, love, loss, joy, suffering, spirituality, death.

Hughes, in 'Cadenza', is particularly Redgrovean, speaking of 'clouds… full of surgery and collision' (*Selected Poems*, 66). And Redgrove would agree with Hughes when the latter writes '[o]nce was every woman the witch' (ib, 56). Hughes employs metaphors that have become the staple diet of modernist poetry; this is from Hughes' 'Cleopatra':

Nile moves in me; my thighs splay
Into the squalled Mediterranean. (ib, 56)

Hughes will write, in 'Pibroch' (from *Wodwo*): '[t]he sea cries with its meaningless voice' (ib, 108). The 'meaningless' quality of the ocean is quite in tune with the outlook of modernism, as found in the Second Law of Thermodynamics, chaos theory, quantum mechanics, Eliot's *The Waste Land*, Beckett's *Waiting For Godot*, Sartre's *Nausea* and the works of Jean Genet, Ionesco, Albert Camus, Aldous Huxley, etc. Redgrove, though, will not write 'meaningless': the word hardly occurs in his *oeuvre*. In 'Relic', from *Lupercal*, Hughes describes trawling the shore and finding bones, shells, skulls, bits of animals; when Redgrove scours the strand he sees things in a much more positive light. Deep negativity, depression and 'dark nights of the soul' rarely occur in Redgrove's poetry. The poem 'The Idea of Entropy at Maenporth Beach', Redgrove says, 'is one of the few poems I think I have let [blackness] come through... where one faces a nothingness anterior to the negotiation.' (MR)

Hughes presents a world of animals and Nature struggling for survival: lambs, ravens, rabbits, pike, salmon, hawks, tigers, their life is lived right in the midst of dust and grime and pain; Redgrove's world is equally founded in actualities, but it is not as bleak, as uncompromising, as ruthless as Hughes' poetic world. While Hughes speaks of skulls and bones, of people and animals as barely more than skeletons, chilled to the bone, Redgrove speaks of skin and warmth, of the synæsthesia of the body. In Hughes' poetry, bodies are halfway butchered, as if hanging up like skinned rabbits; in Redgrove, bodies are not near-dead meat, but living, pulsing things, with orgasmic, euphoric potential.

Hughes and Redgrove share the same view of the basic poetic trance, which Robert Graves wrote about so often. In *Poetry in the Making*, Hughes compared writing poetry to hunting:

> The special kind of excitement, the slightly mesmerized and quite involuntary concentration with which you make out the stirrings of a new poem in your mind, then the outline, the mass and colour and clean final form of it, the unique living reality of it in the midst of general lifelessness, all that is too familiar to mistake. This is hunting and the poem is a new species of creature, a new specimen of the life outside your own.' (17)

Redgrove is sometimes like the novelist J.G. Ballard (born in 1930, he is, like Ted Hughes, Redgrove's contemporary). There is the same idiosyncratic and often bizarre way of experiencing the world. Ballard will speak of the volumes inverting themselves behind someone as they move in a room (in his *The Atrocity Exhibition*, for example).[3] Like Ballard and Hughes, Redgrove also

---
3 J.G. Ballard: *The Atrocity Exhibition*, Panther, 1967

employs heaps of shamanism, post-Jungian psychology and Western mythology. In "The Wedding By the Powerhouse", for instance, Redgrove writes of a shamanic man who can 'sing the clouds away' then 'drove them together with a melodious twang', to make rain' (CM, 36). Redgrove may not like to be associated with Ballard's ruthless and self-conscious postmodernism, but this extract from 'The Silvery Old Goldsmith' shows just how Ballardian Redgrove is, or how Redgrovean Ballard is: the goldsmith, a shamanic and alchemical figure, has made a construction which is

> A tree of spikes of silver
> Set in ebony, say two feet high;
> It was white lightning branching within
> Jet thunder, done
> As a midget's hat-stand: 'It is a model
> To scale of a radio-echo engraving on the sky
> For a split-second all of Chopin's
> Funeral march in the one figure.' (UR, 25)

Influences

Among poetic influences, which are worth little, and only form what we call here the 'outside' biography, Redgrove cites Langland, Eliot, Robert Frost, Edward Thomas and Coleridge. The affinities between Redgrove and nature poets such as Robert Frost, Thomas Hardy and Edward Thomas are obvious. Poems such as 'For the Unfallen' and 'Wild Walls', from *Under the Reservoir* and *In the Hall of the Saurians*, describe nature in detail: spiders, jellyfish, mice, grass and moons. Redgrove departs from the naturalism of Hardy and Thomas when he writes lines such as

Peter Redgrove: Here Comes the Flood

> In my dream-body I enter the earth.
> Perfumes enlarges space, builds boulevards in it;
> I am surrounded by entrances.
> Her excitement is like an apron of waterfall... (UR, 22)

Redgrove admires 'Shakespeare for his eloquence', not for his worldview or his 'atmosphere'.[4] 'For me,' he says, 'the pleasure is not so much in the plot or the politics of the plays, as in the way these people are able to see the world and speak of it directly. There is no inhibition in the speech.' (MR) He appreciates the thoroughly patriarchal Bible for its poetic magic, but not for its morality. 'The Bible has been more important than Shakespeare, because it is introverted and supernatural... The Bible is masculinist, but it is so *full* that it reaches a different dimension through this, as poetry should; and poetry perceives reality' he writes (letter, 14 March 1993). He says he is not influenced by Robert Graves or D.H. Lawrence, but the similarities with his poetry are many.

Lawrence, for instance, wrote in his short stories (and in many others places) of the touch that awakens life. In "A Propos of *Lady Chatterley's Lover*", Lawrence wrote: '[w]e must get back into relation, vivid and nourishing relation to the cosmos' (*Phoenix*, 355). The basic thrust of Lorenzo's philosophy was the struggle into being, into awareness, into a direct relation, or touch, with people and the world. Redgrove's aims, as we shall see, are similar.

---

4 letter to the author, 14 March 1993

Peter Redgrove: Here Comes the Flood

Psychology, Poetics

What this amounts to is a misleading, external biography, a lineage which is not really useful for approaching the real Redgrove. Far more important have been the magical, mythical, psychological and emotional influences. His biggest influence, and the centre of his poetic world, is his wife, Penelope Shuttle. 'The greatest influence is undoubtedly Penelope Shuttle,' he wrote to me.[5]

'Experiences' is a far better term than 'influences', for Redgrove everywhere emphasises the 'experienced'. That is, life as lived in the body, in the flesh, not in the abstract. In his book of programmes written in the 60s for the BBC schools department, which featured a couple of Redgrove's poems, Ted Hughes spoke of poetry as experiences rather than thoughts:

> Poetry is not made out of thoughts or casual fancies. It is made out of experiences which change our bodies, and spirits, whether momentarily or for good. (*Poetry in the Making*, 32)

One must not underestimate the importance of (natural) science in Redgrove's poetic world. Like Hughes, Ballard, Colin Wilson, and many other writers of his generation, Redgrove employs some of the ideas of the New Physics, from quantum mechanics, chaos theory and so on. Light is made up of waves, and so are we: these are the ideas Redgrove explores. Except he will come back to Earth always, and say there are more waves (of light and energy) the ocean than there in the night sky.

His secret, inner lineage stems from Jung, John Layard and Gerald Massey, and others, such as Norman O. Brown, Mantak Chia and Herbert Marcuse, among thinkers.[6] It is possible, for instance, to analyze Redgrove's poesie from a purely Jungian

---
5 letter to the author, ib.
6 see Laz, MR, PR, and other interviews.

standpoint. Alternatively, one might look at Redgrove in terms of feminism, which we do later on. Or in terms of magic – how Redgrove fits in with Western magic, which he draws on. Or New Age thinking. Or the natural sciences. All these strains link up in Redgrove, and the great unifier is of the poet himself.

Penelope Shuttle

It is important too to recognize the significance of Penelope Shuttle in Redgrove's poetic 'mother-world'. As Redgrove writes: 'I used to meet with her at night/ In the scented garden for the blind' ('Visibility Nil', AB, 57). More than any other individual, Shuttle is the Black Goddess, the embodiment for Redgrove of the fantastic feminine (Shuttle has a Black Goddess appearing in her poem 'Leatherman': 'Leatherman has a wife whose skin is black./ She is his black joy./ Her black-skinned body is a gift that she gives and gives.' *Adventures*, 56) Robert Graves had his 'Muse-women', women whom the Goddess used to 'ride' or move in.[7] Graves became besotted, utterly, with his Muse-women, keeping the Muse's love quite separate from marital, domestic love. In Redgrove, there is no separation of domesticity and spirituality, for the Muse is right inside the family home, setting it alight with her ever-changing menstrual weather. Redgrove's life revolves around Shuttle, artistically, spiritually, socially, – you name it. As Redgrove says 'I'm sure I'd rather be her than myself' (Hud, 378).

---

[7] on Graves and his 'Muse-women', see Jeremy Robinson: *Blinded By Her Light: The Love-Poetry of Robert Graves*, Crescent Moon 1991; Patrick Keane: *A Wild Civility: Interactions in the Poetry and Thought of Robert Graves*, University of Missouri Press, Columbia 1980; *Conversations With Robert Graves*, University of Mississippi Press, Jackson 1989

Shuttle is at the centre of Redgrove's poetic life, much as Laura was at the heart of Petrarch's poetic life, or Beatrice was at the heart of Dante's poetic life. Shuttle is one of the inspirations (as well as one of the saints) for such marvellous lines in Redgrove as:

> The cloud-flower born of flowers in a flower-shape at flower-time.
> (from 'Superstition',WNP, 98)

Shuttle's poems are intimate and close-up, spiralling inwards more often than outwards. Redgrove writes: 'Penelope's work is less strident than mine, and she tends to build up a loving impression rather than voyage through the whole universe, as I seem to.'[8] You can't tell Redgrove and Shuttle apart sometimes: they work together a good deal.[9] 'The works of both of us are by our Magical Child...so there will be resemblances, especially in that the world is presented transformed and nearer its actuality, a reality discerned by our sexual workings' writes Redgrove (letter, 20 July 1992). The 'Magical Child' is a term in sexual alchemy. Shuttle and Redgrove use the symbol of the alchemical 'double pelican' to show how they initiate, feed and exchange essences, energies, experiences, poetry and magic with each other. Redgrove writes that the 'point of the Double Pelican is that we initiate each other; and since we are both artists we are able to do this on several levels'.[10] Penelope Shuttle explains further:

> Intimacy then in our relationship pivots on three elements in our shared reality: poetry; sex; Cornwall. But how do two people write, man and woman, when they write both their collaborative works and their own works? Imagine it to be like the alchemical double pelican; one person reads the other one's work and absorbs it into themselves, like the child of the pelican feeding from the blood of the maternal breast; then, nourished by the work, that writer will write; and in turn offer that work back to the partner, offering the sustained

---

8 letter, 20 July 1992
9 see Erika Duncan: *We Two*; MR; Laz; Hud; *The Wise Wound*, etc
10 letter, 14 April 1993

breast on which the other may feed; this continues, this giving and taking of nourishment... In some works, the collaborative works, the page will be shared between us; ideas and images flowing through; in the separate works, the other will be there like an invisible spirit animating the work. Thus we are contained one in the other; sharing the same reality; this is an alchemical interchange. (We, 126)

Generally, Shuttle's poems are concentrated, compressed, meticulously crafted and woven, spun out of the fine membranes of womb-tissue. They are poems in which extraordinary events occur in the body, not on the gargantuan scale of 'masculine' subjects such as battles, politics, international communications. Shuttle's poetry is an art where whispers can be more powerful than a scream, where 'a private endearment is stronger/ than the roar of prayer' ('Dark-Room', *The Child-Stealer*, 37). Poems such as 'The Weather House' are more Redgrovean than Redgrove's own poems ('we build our weather house/ from the shaking white boughs of electricity', *The Lion From Rio*, 6). In 'Ancient Geographers', Shuttle writes in a Redgrovean manner of 'the strong excitement/ of cloud and dark coming on' at twilight (*Orchard*, 7).

Shuttle has spoken of living in Falmouth as being surrounded by water, just as Redgrove has done, a place where a shell is a 'hydrophone,/ A seaphone or oceanophone or abyssophone' (A, 8). The poem 'Breath' directly recalls Redgrove's 'Living in Falmouth' and other poems, where the Carrick Roads and the Atlantic Ocean are the primary environment of the Cornish town.

Shuttle has written a number of love poems which are more ferocious than Redgrove's, and read something like Ted Hughes' violent, sensual pieces (for example, Shuttle's poem 'Clayman, Leatherman and Glassman').

Redgrove is hardly ever this explicit. Shuttle gleefully and lovingly describes all the physical facts of lovemaking. The narrator of *The Sleep of the Great Hypnotist* makes love ecstatically with a menstrual woman, having visions as he does so. After the orgasm, the woman asks 'did you see my Devil?' and thanks him: 'Thank you, Satan, thank you.' (65-66) Allusions are made to hallucinogens and the witches' practice of riding the broomstick. Redgrove does allow himself to be exuberantly orgasmic in the prose piece "Dance the Putrefact", in *From Every Chink of the Ark*, and included in the novel *The Facilitators*, where the narrator enmeshes with the Black Goddess in a multi-sensory mudbath:

> I am down, and within her! I have vaulted into her boundaries and I am as black as she is. I am buried deep in her flesh. I pull her flesh off her in handfuls and cover my skin in hers. I prance, cool and nightladen with exterior cunt. The black bed before me is rucked. The black woman-outline has risen from it and I dance within her skin. I am the black woman. I am petal-soft, and my surfaces are rounded and shining. The bosom of my shirt is heavy with mud. It hangs and flounces like large breasts full of black milk. The black lady minces sadly loverless over the mud, she smells of tar and sunlight. Where is this white lover? She dances sadly on her own. Soon her lover will return, but her disappearance is the condition of his return. She will enjoy the sunlight while she can. Soon her ladyhood will pour like black blood through the drains of his bathroom, she will fade like a shadow in a shower of clear water. (CM, 61)

Shuttle's fullest and most detailed depiction of lovemaking is 'Act of Love', which is a wildly sexual piece, full of animals, motion, darkness and violence. It is a record of a 'hauntingly-real fuck' (*Lion*, 30), and contains some magnificent lines, such as: 'a labour of love as we rush towards that trembling edge' (everyone knows about running to the edge and leaping off it during lovemaking), and 'we are gasping to smell the sleep to come' (ib., 31).

'Nuptial Arts' is another evocation of orgasmic bliss, in which the storm in the bed equals and surpasses the thunderstorm outside, in nature. Not all of Shuttle's poems are of this kind, though the woman on top of the man in sex occurs frequently in

Shuttle (in 'Trick Horse', for example), recalling the Indian Goddess Kali who makes love to her consorts on top – and then decapitates them.[11] Shuttle's 'Trick Horse' depicts sex in Tantric terms, as a Tantric, religious experience, yet wholly natural.

Shuttle, though, is not particularly interested in the negative themes that are discussed by feminists, Lacanians and Freudians (Hélène Cixous, Juliet Mitchell, Luce Irigaray, Julia Kristeva, Toril Moi, among others). She is more interested in birth than death, as the many poems concerning pregnancy, labour and delivery show ('The Child-Stealer', 'Mother and Child', 'Intimate Sketch', 'Seventh Son', 'Zoe's Horse', 'Home Birth' and 'Delicious Babies'). As with Redgrove, birth for Shuttle is a wet, erotic experience, verily The Flood. In 'Mountain' the narrator kisses a young midwife hungrily, aroused by his wife's labour. For Shuttle, as for Redgrove, sexuality is all liquid, so that kisses make rain, and lovemaking creates The Flood. Shuttle has written poems that come from the same 'mother-world' as the Redgroverse. Such as in 'Passion', where lovemaking is an alchemical ferment, like burning up in an alchemical vessel, as if the lovers were the twin dragons of alchemy, one green and one gold, going through the *rubedo* of alchemy in a room that becomes a huge alchemical vessel. Like Petrarch in so many of the sonnets in the *Rime Sparse*, Shuttle contrasts fire with ice, in the best sonneteering tradition, and in part two of 'Passion' has the lover as ice: '[h]is sex is a prism of ice in me' (*Adventures*, 26)

As with Redgrove, Shuttle includes many synæsthetic elements in her poesie: the taste of milk, the heady smells of sex ('her petalled ovarian smell' in 'Her Butterfly Husband'), the

---

[11] Wendy O'Flaherty writes: 'The Goddess not only dominates her consort but kills him, cutting off his head. In this she resembles the female praying mantis, who bites off her consort's head... By eating his head, the mantis removes her consort's inhibitions and frees him to copulate more vigorously.' *Women, Androgynes, and other Mythical Beasts*, University of Chicago Press, Chicago, 1980, 81

touch of a cow's 'blowzy tough rosy udders' ('Jungian Cows', *Adventures*, 1), the feel of sticky thighs ('Honeymoon', *Taxing*, 36). Hers is a poetry founded on the body, on the weathers and seasons – and visions and phantasies - of the body.

She writes too of menstruation, childbirth, pregnancy, subjects considered 'women's mysteries'. In 'The Conceiving' she addresses her unborn child: '[n]ow you are here/ you worker in the gold of flesh' (*Orchard*, 44). But Shuttle treats 'women's mysteries' as wholly natural, not 'mysterious', even though these experiences retain their mystery, their amazing qualities. The child in the womb is both an everyday occurrence, and an extraordinary thing. *This child in my body*, how can pregnancy be otherwise than utterly astonishing? Yet, Shuttle writes of being pregnant as a wholly natural situation. This blend of magic and everydayness is displayed here in 'Maritimes' in a straightforward fashion. For Redgrove, the ordinary is magical, and magic is quite ordinary, so Redgrove doesn't like the word 'magic', because it suggests there is something too special about magic, whereas Redgrove believes it should be accessible to all. Magic can be applied to pregnancy too, and in *The Sleep of the Great Hypnotist* Pfoundes discussing methods of hypnosis which allow the woman to 'consciously discover the way her organs developed and acted in preparation for and during childbirth' (SGH, 34). Here, Shuttle treats pregnancy as simultaneously mysterious and everyday, and makes the age-old connections between the ocean and mothers, between the primaeval mother of us all, the sea as Goddess, and herself, pregnant, going for a swim. Poems such as 'At Perranporth, March 1976' are directly comparable with Redgrove's 'The Moon Disposes'. In poems such as 'Candle on a Rainy Morning', Shuttle comes across as a Redgrovean poet (or is it that Redgrove is a Shuttlean poet?).

In 'Overnight', Shuttle again trawls subject matter that Redgrove has made his own: wet clothes. But Shuttle is of course the inspiration for Redgrove's explorations of the erotic, fetishistic nature of wet shirts. As Shuttle knows, the skin is the most erotic of all the garments humans wear. In 'Overnight', Shuttle makes the connections, so familiar in Redgrove's poetry, between rain and orgasms, so that rainfall is a 'skin-orgasm', as Redgrove calls it. Indeed, it is difficult to know who invents what in Shuttle's and Redgrove's poetry, because the 'skin-orgasm', like so much else, is a feature of both their work. It may be that Shuttle 'writes' much of Redgrove's work, either directly or indirectly. Certainly she influences much of it. Feminists have noted that Jessie Chambers was responsible for some of D.H. Lawrence's ideas; he used his female friends as sources of information on women, feminists have said. In the same way, Shuttle may provide Redgrove with some of his ideas. It doesn't matter. Redgrove has always acknowledged Shuttle's presence in his work. He's said he'd like to be her, at times. In the alchemical 'double pelican' scenario, which is the model Shuttle and Redgrove use for their relationship, the two writers become interchangeable. Questions of authorship become no longer important. The work becomes a continuum, flowing freely from Shuttle to Redgrove. Muse and poet become one.

Nature, Mysticism, Cornwall

Some critics see Redgrove as a nature mystic. Certainly, there is an amazingly powerful and elemental sense of Nature in his works. We might cite British poets such as George Herbert, Henry Vaughan, William Blake and William Wordsworth as precursors of Redgrovean nature mysticism – these poets are behind Ted

Hughes too, as they form the backbone of the British nature poetry tradition. Think of Henry Vaughan's 'night' poems, which speak of the dazzling darkness, where eternity lives and breathes.

Redgrove diverges from nature mystics in their pantheist doctrine of God-in-nature, as espoused by mystics such as Meister Eckhart, John Smith, Jeffries and Wordsworth. Jacob Boehme is typical when he writes: '[i]n this light my spirit saw through all things and into all creatures, and I recognized God in grass and plants.'[12]

For Redgrove, Nature is so extraordinary, it doesn't require a deity to make it extraordinary. Nature already is extraordinary, and Nature don't need no God to make it like that. At the same time, there is a religious aspect to Redgrove, for he exalts the Goddess, as Robert Graves does. Marina Warner writes: 'as with another magus, Robert Graves, the feminine for Redgrove is a source of spiritual energy which men may tap for their own health, and he advocates a form of material mysticism mediated through female bodies.' Redgrove goes for the Black Goddess, the dark side of the deity, but the deification is none the less powerful and religious as it is in mediæval mystics.

The Duchy, whether it's the ancient granite seabound Celtic kingdom or the modern seaside holiday resort, exerts a powerful influence on Redgrove. Redgrove's poems have many aspects of Cornwall in them, not only in obvious ways (in 'Falmouth Clouds', 'Ghostly Town' or 'Cornwall Honeymoon'), but also in so much of the imagery, the feelings and the underlife of magic. Like the Elizabethans in their pastoral lyrics, when they are speaking of love and 'shepherdesses' in the landscape, Redgrove's poems are full of sunshine, rain, wind, clouds, the panoply of natural elements. In pastoral poetry, though, in Spenser's *The Shepheardes Calendar* and the Arcadian paeans of

---

[12] Jacob Boehme, quoted in John Ferguson, 130

Michael Drayton, Samuel Daniel, Robert Herrick and Philip Sidney, the clouds, rain, sunlight and trees can be seen as metaphors or symbols of something else. Redgrove, though, sidesteps metaphor, going for the heart of the experience. He dives deeper than metaphor, and although he employs many analogies and comparisons, this is because he is interested in the thing in itself. Lacking a descriptive language, he tries all manner of comparisons, using many 'likes' and 'as ifs', in order to point the reader closer and closer to the actual thing-in-itself.

Redgrove has included most of Cornwall in his poems: the gardens of Tresco on the Scilly Isles; Penzance; Land's-End; Falmouth (the docks, Swanpool, Maenporth beach, the harbour, the library, etc); Truro; Padstow, a favourite Cornish town for Redgrove (not least for its celebrated Maytime festival, when the 'Obby 'Oss and the Teazer dance through the streets – Redgrove has written a radio play on this theme, and the pagan festival features in *The Sleep of the Great Hypnotist*); Boscastle (for the Museum of Witchcraft); Perranporth; Zennor; the Poldark Mine at Helston, and so on.

Poems such as 'The Alchemical Honeymoon', 'Weather Begins Here', 'Living in Falmouth', 'Raven at Goonhillie', 'The Moons of Scilly', 'Grimmanderson on Tresco', 'Minerals of Cornwall, Stones of Cornwall', 'Round Pylons' and 'The Moon Disposes' are flooded with Cornish imagery and themes. 'The Alchemical Honeymoon' brings together the perennial Redgrovean poetic realms: alchemy and magic, Cornwall and landscape, love and eroticism, and a generous sensuality: it serves as good introduction to Redgrove's poetic world:

> The fatness of the ocean: the
> Opulence of the earth: the groom appears,
> The bronze man, so tanned it's green
>
> Or a hint of green, as the folios wish.

Peter Redgrove: Here Comes the Flood

> The chymical embrace in the bath, the rainbow
> Vessel, the foaming bathsalt
>
> Of four colours.

The point about Peter Redgrove's Cornwall is that it is a magical place. In seemingly humdrum towns such as Penzance and Falmouth there are extraordinary alchemical events occurring. Even in the would-be genteel, chintzy *Vogue, Lady* and *Tatler* interiors and the National Trust country houses and gardens with their cream teas amazing things happen. In Redgrove, Cornwall becomes as marvellous as China, India, Russia or South America. His magic realism (or realistic magic) makes the most dull place luminous. He would find the pulse of the natural world even in a square foot of turf resting on the dirty windowsill of a derelict factory in a run-down inner city wasteland. The poem 'National Trust' captures this larger world amidst the everyday world vividly, where the denizens of the sleepy holiday destinations in the West Country are living in a quivering world of superabundance, if only they were alive to it:

> All the trees had rounded their flanks like great homes,
> Like great lungs smelling of grass, like magical robes,
> Delicious garments that are green with many tabs
>
> And fruiting buttons, with seams all lined with flowers,
> Garments grown, not made, the most humane of clothes.
> (Man, 48-49)

The whole point of Redgrove's poetic vision is that when you look really closely at things, they become amazing. You just have to look closely, carefully, in a relaxed but attentive, calm but perceptive state of mind. Thus, sand, which seems to be dull brown all over, is in fact made up all manner of colours. When you look close enough, as the painter really studies the world, you see the extraordinary range of colours in seemingly dull and ordinary things like sand and soil:

> Each palmful, lens-inspected, is a spectrum of their colours which in the larger scale and look of distance dissolve to this dune-beige. There plays over these grosser visible registers of small ridge, hollowed dry wave, the implicit spectrum which I have held in the palm of my hand; thus are the levels joined. Clear shards, orange stars, droplets of red iron ore, citrine seeds, greenstones, transparent anvils of quartz and amethyst, granite grains (hovis-coloured) and the sudden amazement of a spiral shell like an empty castle... (MFT, 19-20)

Lean close and you see the wonder, says Redgrove. The wonder of the microcosmic realm reflects the wonder of the macrocosmic. In this extract from 'The Yoniversity at Rock', Redgrove describes the wonder of the sand dunes near Padstow.

Penelope Shuttle speaks of three things important in her relationship with Redgrove: love, poetry and Cornwall,[13] and Cornwall is crucial in Redgrove's poetic world. It is the Cornwall of constantly changing weather, of clouds and storms and bees and estuaries and dunes and, of course, the sea, always the sea, on all sides, always moving, the rhythm of the tides invading the coastal stretches. 'Water murmurs in all created things' says Redgrove in a poem, 'Oceanophone' (*Abyssophone*, 8). Redgrove calls it 'the dreaming sea', in so many poems, and of course it is the (symbol of) restless unconscious *par excellence,* and it feeds his poetry endlessly.

The poem 'Sunlight, Moonlight, Stonelight' identifies in its title the subjects of the poem, but misses out that all-important Cornish element, the sea. We must add 'sealight' or 'oceanlight' to the natural elements that are self-illumined here. For, as Redgrove writes here, '[t]he sea contains more lights/ Than the sky does' (IHS, 48). In 'Sunlight, Moonlight, Stonelight' Redgrove

---

[13] Penelope Shuttle, talking of 'a threefold reality: of poetry: of love, erotic, spiritual...and of Cornwall (not England), weather and landscape and separateness' (*We Two*, 12)

speaks of that luminosity which is within things. This is one way of speaking about the 'essence of things'. Constantin Brancusi the sculptor spoke of 'essences', and his stone and marble sculptures *Fish, Seal, The Beginning of the World* and *Prometheus* shine with an inner light. Similarly, Lawrence Durrell spoke many times of the dancing, electrical blue light of Greece. In 'Sunlight, Moonlight' Stonelight', Redgrove says, rightly, that '[t]here is light within', and his evocation of 'self-lighted stones' would seem apposite a description to anyone who has seen those smooth, round white granite stone on beaches of Cornwall. And, though he is writing of the Scilly Isles here, as in other poems (such as one of his very best, 'Grimmanderson on Tresco'), the Scillies here can represent all of Cornwall, even though they are a quite distinct part of it:

> A heath of turf that bows to the sea at night,
> A webwork of sunshine in which the islands are caught;
> A black cliff still as a sleeping medium throws out its white cloud-
>   ghost
> Miles into the air. The sea contains more lights
> Than the sky does, by millions, in fractured waves. (IHS, 48)

The Alchemical Journal (entitled *In the Esplumeor* in *The Cyclopean Mistress*) is particularly deeply soaked in Cornish imagery and experiences. In no.33, Redgrove describes one of the mines, near Helston. Mines, and their glittering minerals, feature a good deal in Redgrove's poetry (in 'Minerals of Cornwall, Stones of Cornwall', for example). Jewels can be wombs too: '[w]henever you see a diamond,' writes Redgrove in *The Guest Father*, 'suspect a yoni. Diamond-Goddess of the World.' (GF, 28) In the 'womb' of the Earth, to use an age-old poetic metaphor, alchemical transformations can occur. Redgrove's *In the Esplumeor* is a paean to the fecundity of the Earth, embodied in the dark spaces of the mines:

> Under the black light, mother and daughter, in Poldark Mine, near Helston, the room lined with shelves full of the crystalline minerals bathed in ultra-violet, shining their unnamed colours, like solid fireworks slowly exploding, the mother and daughter, the faces black but the radiant white calcite of the teeth luminous as the million year lump of calcite aglow beside them, the light's tunes played on the rocks, the nails bright in the black hands like night reaching out of the bluely-luminous ocean-foaming sleeves.

Redgrove's nature poems, then, might be seen as poems of Cornwall. Cornwall of course is a little world or kingdom in itself, quite distinct from the rest of Britain. It is a wild place – in summer or winter. The tourists don't know the wildness of the Cornish winter on the north coasts, but they know the sudden Cornish mists that come down out of nowhere. The wheeling, sqwarking seagulls. The old stone walls. The tors. The extraordinary flora and fauna (especially on the Lizard peninsula). Boats parked on the roads, sand kicked over the tarmac. The clanking of ropes and masts in the harbours. Penelope Shuttle describes West Cornwall thus:

> West Penwith is high moorland: gorse; heather; bracken; some cultivated tracts of land; rocky outcrops, ancient stones, ever-changing shades and shadows of sea, sky and land... It was a different land, having a profound stillness of earth, of stone, and a glittering lurching light from sea and sky; an enclave agitated yet peaceful, simmering yet stable; changing and unchanging, a place of second and third and fourth thoughts, on to infinity. (We, 123)

Painting

Paul Theroux says somewhere that the north coast of Cornwall, with its white Atlantic waves rolling in, its craggy cliffs and bracing wind, is as wild as anywhere in the world. In Cornwall, you can turn a corner, even in the busiest touristy towns, and suddenly be in a quiet, isolated space. It is this combination of seclusion, light, weather, stony earth, history and many other elements that attracts people to Cornwall. The artists who worked in Cornwall – Barbara Hepworth, Bernard Leach, Peter Lanyon, Patrick Heron, Naum Gabo, Ben Nicholson, etc – formed a colony much celebrated in art criticism. The abstract landscape painting tradition is still strong in Cornwall. Some of Redgrove's poems can be seen as poetic equivalents of the abstract painterly tradition. For occasionally Redgrove attempts a portrait of Cornwall that seems particularly painterly, such as 'Raven at Goonhillie':

> A pallid straw-field of stubble,
> A bleached field,
> A raven stalking through
> ...It is said
> A raven is born
> Every time it thunders
> Over the wheat-fields
> Golden as kippers (IHS, 46-7)

Poems such as 'Opulent' and 'Minerals of Cornwall, Stones of Cornwall' mix the usual landscape/ holiday elements of Cornwall – mines, quarries, minerals, stone, ocean, gulls, moors – but with Redgrove's fine, synæsthetic and sometimes peculiar perception. Redgrove's Cornwall is no static, unchanging place, but a vibrant and continually mutating landscape, always interacting with humans. Mineshafts in Redgrove, for instance, are not simply ruined holes in the ground ringed by fences with DANGER signs stuck on them, they are flumes exuding secret perfumes:

> I move to the open shaft
> To inhale the deep breath
> Out of the lungs of this mine. (FE, 53)

The ancestors of Redgrove's affinities with painting are not, however, Peter Lanyon, Ben Nicholson or Patrick Heron, but the Surrealists, and in particular the women Surrealists, Remedios Varo, Leonor Fini, Meret Oppenheim, Leonora Carrington, Dorothea Tanning and Frida Kahlo. It is these women Surrealists, rather than Dali, Magritte, Ernst and Tanguy, that resonate in Redgrove's poetry. Paintings by Kahlo and Varo appear on the covers of Redgrove's *The Cyclopean Mistress* and *Selected Poems*.

The spaces of the women Surrealists of the 30s, 40s and 50s are the spaces of dreams and the unconscious, places where private and mythic images coalesce, as in more recent women's art, such as Rachel Whiteread's rooms, or the bizarre installations of Judy Pfaff. Leonora Carrington paints the clean, empty rooms of the unconscious, populated by bizarre items, bizarre partly for their juxtapositioning with other objects,[14] such as in her *Self-Portrait*.[15] Dorothea Tanning, for so long known simply as 'the wife of a famous artist' (Max Ernst), also painted fantastic dreamscapes, places where shapes merge into shapes in flowing streams of energy, in the Redgrovean manner, such as in her visionary *Guardian Angels*, or where young women – again, as in Fini and Carrington, with long, wild hair – encounter gigantic yellow sunflowers on mysterious hotel landings, as in *Eine Kleine*

---

[14] See Juan Garcia Ponce & Leonora Carrington: *Leonora Carrington*, Mexico City 1974; Edward James, intr, *Leonora Carrington*, Center for Inter-American Relations, New York 1975; Gloria Orenstein: "Leonora Carrington's Visionary Art for the New Age", *Chrysalis*, 4, 1978, 65-77
[15] Carrington: *Self-Portrait*, 1936-7, oil on canvas, 25.5 x 32in, Pierre Matisse Gallery, New York

Nachtmusik.[16] For strangeness, the images of women Surrealists far surpass those of the male artists. They celebrate strange as Redgrove does.

Take the work of Remedios Varo, the painter who is perhaps most approximates to Redgrove's poetic vision. Like Fini, Carrington and Tanning, Varo creates the rooms of dreams, those spacious spaces that haunt the viewer with their extraordinary perspectives and contents.[17] Varo's paintings are furnished with bizarre machines out of Jean Tinguely, objects that Redgrove delights in describing, such as in his 'The Silvery Old Goldsmith', or in the prose piece "How Much For the Box?", which describes an object Varo might have painted:

> Inside the case was a slab of ebony: black, polished wood. Set in a hollow of this was a silver object, conical, resembling a pear, or perhaps a stylised heart. There was an opening in the front of this object: it was hollow, and lined with a fine red velvet. (CM, 27))

Remedios Varo's *Creation of the Birds* seems particularly Redgrovean: we see a bird woman (a female shaman) making birds with the aid of the light of a distant star focused through a prism, a machine which looks like two eggs on top of each that dispenses paint, and a paint brush connected to a violin. The painting fuses the magic of light, music and colour in an alchemical fantasy of creation, as in *Harmony*, where a poet, aided by supernatural Muses, composes art on a luminous, three dimensional musical stave.[18] Like Redgrove's poetry, Remedios

---

16 Dorothea Tanning: *Eine Kleine Nachtmusik*, 1946, oil on canvas, 16.2 x 24in, private collection; *Guardian Angels*, 1946, oil on canvas, 48 x 55in, New Orleans Museum of Art, New Orleans

17 See Octavio Paz & Roger Callois: *Remedios Varo*, Mexico City 1973; Edouard Jaguer: *Remedios Varo*, Paris 1980; *Remedios Varo*, Museo de Arte Moderno, Mexico City 1983

18 Remedios Varo: *Creation of the Birds*, 1958, oil on masonite, 20.6 x 24.6in, private collection; *Harmony*, 1956, oil on masonite, 30 x 37in, private collection

Varo's paintings are based on an alchemical view of the world, where all things are related in a holistic continuum. 'Varo believed in magic. She had an animistic faith in the power of objects and in the interrelatedness of plant, animal, human, and mechanical worlds,' writes Janet Kaplan.[19] The most celebrated female Surrealist is Frida Kahlo, whose amazing self-portraits with their cutaway images of her body, are among the most ruthless explorations of sexuality in modern 'high art'.[20] Kahlo and Redgrove explore the invisible workings of the body, although Kahlo's art has an element of self-hatred not found in Redgrove's work. Kahlo's *The Broken Column, The Two Fridas,* and the astonishing *My Birth,* investigate forms of (female) suffering, the relation of sexuality to violence, sexuality to self-image, sexuality to emotions (hatred, self-loathing, insecurity, rage).[21] By contrast, Redgrove's images are of healing and tenderness, where the feminine is exalted, and self-torture is far-off.

---

19 J. Kaplan: "Remedios Varo: Voyages and Visions:, *Woman's Art Journal*, 1, no.2, Autumn 1980/ Winter 1981, 13
20 see Hayden Herrera: *Frida: A Biography of Frida Kahlo*, Harper & Row, New York 1983; "Frida Kahlo: Her Life, Her Art", *Artforum*, 14, May 1976, 38-4; Gloria Orenstein: "Frida Kahlo: Painting For Miracles", *Feminist Art Journal*, Autumn 1973, 7-9; Terry Smith: "From the Margins: Modernity and the Case of Frida Kahlo", *Block*, 8, 1983, 14
21 Frida Kahlo: *My Birth*, oil on sheet metal, 12.2 x 14in, collection: Edgar J. Kaufmann, New York; *The Broken Column*, 1944, oil on masonite, 15.8 x 12.2in, collection: Dolores Olmedo, Mexico City; *The Two Fridas*, 1939, oil on canvas, 67 x 67in, Museo de Arte Moderno, Mexico City

Two

Alchemy of the Word: Peter Redgrove's Poetics

Another sense centres into my synthesis,
For my machines with intricate induction-coils
In their fresh-generated sparks

Smell of the German forests, home of Romanticism.
It is as though I experiment within
A roaring waterfall smelling of green pine,

And with my nose clean and my catarrah dried up
I can enjoy the interior of my skull
Like a Frankenstein Castle at last.

Peter Redgrove, 'The Monster-Scent' (*Abyssophone*, 24)

Redgrove, Rilke, Rimbaud and the Romantics

If I put Redgrove into a poetic tradition, it is that of the Romantics, first of all, and the German Romantics in particular: Goethe especially, and Novalis (the hermetic Novalis of *Hymns to the Night*) and Hölderlin. Novalis created a powerful transcendent poetry, a mixture of poetry and philosophy, which he called 'magisch', 'Magie', his 'magic idealism' (*Works*, III). He has some wonderful things to say about poetry, and its relation to life, such as:

> Poetry is what is truly and absolutely real, this is the kernel of my philosophy. The more poetic, the more true. (*Works*, III, 11)

> In the essential sense, philosophizing is - a caress - a testimony to the inner love of reflection, the absolute delight of wisdom. (*Pollen*, 53)

> All absolute sensation is religious. (197)

> To enliven all is the aim of life. (*Pollen*, 64).

> All is seed. (*Pollen*, 73)

> All must become nourishment... Everything can become magical-work. (*Pollen*, 65, 73)

Of course everything should become 'magical-work', and Novalis' magical view of life is that of Redgrove, for whom life is extraordinary – if we are attuned to experiencing it that way. 'Poetry can remind us how extraordinary the ordinary is; that what we see as familiar is also present in a dimension of wonder' writes Penelope Shuttle (We, 1270. The poet who sums up the essence of German Romanticism in the 20th century, Rilke, is a key poet in Redgrove's poetics. So many of Redgrove's ideas chime with those of Rilke. The notion of a vast inner world, for instance, is crucial to Rilke and Redgrove. It is what they found their poetry on. As Novalis writes: '[w]hat is outside me, is really within me, is mind – and vice versa' (*Novalis Schriften,* 3, 429)

For Rilke, poetry is a means of exploring and activating the inner spaces. So Rilke speaks continually in terms of 'Kunst-Ding', of 'essence', space and darkness (the philosophy of innerness and isness outlined in his *Neue Gedichte*). In Rilke, everything is expanding – but not outside, inside, in those dark, windy spaces populated by the Rilkean Angel, that marvellous being which achieved the shamanic journey of moving between this world and the invisible world. As Novalis wrote: '[t]he sorcerer is a poet. The prophet is to the sorcerer as the man of taste is to the poet...The genuine poet is all-knowing' (*Pollen*, 50-51).

Rilke takes his poetics largely from the Symbolists – from Mallarmé in particular, and from Valéry. For Mallarmé, words were magic stuff for achieving a musical solidification of the mysterious invisible. Verlaine and Mallarmé emphasized the concreteness of words, as did Karl Kraus and Ludwig Wittgenstein (albeit in a different way). Redgrove too stresses the actuality of his poetry, the very feel of lines and rhythms. Looking at the poems, you might think they tend towards prose. But each line is carefully worked out, even so. As Eva Salzman writes: 'Redgrove has a certain reputation for writing too much.' She adds: 'I, for one, forgive him his excesses; in fact, I positively love them.' Norman Jope, too, forgives Redgrove his excesses: 'In the last resort, however, I would give him the benefit of the doubt.'

Transformation is Rilke's goal. We must be

> Transformed? Yes, for our task is to stamp this provisional, perishing earth into ourselves so deeply, so painfully and passionately, that its being may rise again, "invisibly", in us. (*Duino Elegies*, 157)

All you have to do in life is to be, just *be*, says Rilke: 'all we basically have to do is to *be*, but simply, earnestly, the way the earth simply is' he wrote in *Letters on Cézanne*. Rilke developed

Mallarmé's ideas. Rilke wrote: '[a] poem enters into language from within, in an aspect forever averted from us. It fills the language wondrously, rising to its very brim'.[22] Like Redgrove, Rilke believes in the supernatural power of poetry to grasp the synæsthetic experiences of life which surrounds us continually, which are flowing over us all the time.[23] Redgrove calls this magical apprehension natural, not supernatural, and Rilke is often much more wistfully mystical than Redgrove. 'Redgrove's mythologising imagination is convincing,' writes Pascale Petit, 'because he utilises the natural forces of the known world and amplifies them to the supersensory degree of animal perceptions' (in *Poetry London Newsletter*). 'Nature becomes hyper-nature in a Redgrove poem, transcending the deadening objectivity of superficial perception and classification, opening itself (and the reader) up to the subtlest emanations, the sweat and breath of the earth' writes Martin Hibbert (30). 'I'm a materialist, you see, but I'm a materialist in the Hindu tradition, which regards matter as a song' says Redgrove in *The Hudson Review* (382). Redgrove's 'celebratory materialism' is problematic for some (David Kennedy, 90), while others claim his 'singing materialism' is 'ultimately optimistic' (O'Donoghue).

Redgrove, though, is fully in accord with Rilke when the poet writes in his marvellous *Sonnets to Orpheus,* one of the very best and most deeply lyrical of all poetic sequences, a series of sonnets which not only prove that the sonnet can still be a powerful form, but that some of the shortest poems can be the most profound:

> What infinity!
> Can't you feel inside your mouth a growing
> mysteriousness, and, where words were, a flowing
> of suddenly released discovery?[24]

---

22 Rilke: *Letters to Benvenuta*, tr Heinz Norden, Hogarth Press, 1953, 51
23 Rilke, "Primal Sound", in H.M. Block & H. Salinger, eds: *The Creative Vision: Modern European Writers*, Grove Press, New York 1960, 50
24 Rilke: *Sonnets to Orpheus*, tr J.B. Leishman, Hogarth Press 1946, 59

Peter Redgrove: Here Comes the Flood

This mystical expansion, of fruit inside the mouth, is something Redgrove could relate to, for his poetry works on this concrete, fleshly level (for instance in the apple/ perfume/ whirlwind/ ripeness sequence in *In the Country of the Skin,* 17). Rilke's sense of space is unparalleled in poetry (see his 'The Bowl of Roses', for instance, which talks so lyrically about the self-illumined Within).[25] Rilke makes mysticism sensual, as Nietzsche did, speaking of infinity as fruit in the mouth. Simple things are enough for Rilke and Redgrove: wind, night, flowers, the sea. The line '[e]verything/ Inside us begins to rejoice' in 'More Than Meets the Eye' is very Rilkean (Tar, 25). It is a line that Rilke wrote often, in one form or another (especially in the *Sonnets to Orpheus*). But what makes Redgrove rejoice? Simple pleasures: a flower, night, perfumes, movement:

> The flower welds
> Its petals together for the night, a little seed
> Of nectar spurts from a gland and glows
> Within its dark pavilion. Everything
> Inside us begins to rejoice. There is a soft
> Milky breath from this well. (Tar, 25)

Redgrove is a firm believer in the fundamentally magical aspect of poetry, its ability to conjure up experiences, so that the poem becomes an experience in itself, not simply a description of an experience. This is a key ethic in post-Symbolist poetics: that the poem itself is an experience. As Rilke put it, 'song is existence', where poetry is life itself, and making poetry is not a commentary 'about' life, but is life itself. This feeling about poetry recalls the *alchuringa* mythic dream-time of the Australian aborigines, where the world is sung into existence (a notion also found in Western occultism, in the 'music of the spheres' of

---
25 Rilke: 'The Bowl of Roses', in *New Poems,* tr J.B. Leishman, Hogarth Press, 1963, 57

hermetic philosophy).[26]

As Redgrove says, 'the purpose of art is to inspire us with our own creative energies' (SS) That is, art makes life, gives life. Redgrove says: 'in Jungian psychology, the end of analysis or the purpose of analysis is to live in a state of active imagination. In other words, to see the correspondences.' (SS) For a time, when he was 16 or so, until he was 19, art was crucial for the psychic well-being of the ever-restless Arthur Rimbaud, another of Redgrove's 'influences'. Rimbaud was the amazing poet who escaped from the utterly bland provincial town of Charleville in North France to wander the streets of Paris in poverty. After writing his *Illuminations* and *A Season in Hell*, the most extraordinary poems of French – and world – literature, Rimbaud renounced it all for a hellish and profoundly boring life in Aden. 'Mortel, ange ET demon, autant dire Rimbaud,' as Rimbaud's lover, Verlaine wrote ('Mortal, angel AND demon, that is to say Rimbaud'.)[27]

Rimbaud is the tornado of world poetry. He outblasts just about every other poet. For poets, he is more significant than the so-called 'founding fathers of the 20th century: Marx, Freud, Nietzsche and Einstein. For other poets, he is 'everybody's favourite hippy', a Communard, a 'precursor of the current movement of subversion of Western notions of self, society, and discourse'[28] or a savage mystic.[29] For Redgrove, Rimbaud became his spiritual guide, his Virgil: 'Rimbaud escorted me many times through Hell and back again' writes Redgrove in "Rimbaud My Virgil" (Rim, 172).

---

21 see James Cowan: *The Mysteries of the Dream-Time*, Prism Press 1989; Bruce Chatwin: *The Songlines*, Picador, 1988; Lucien Lévy-Bruhl: *Primitive Mythology*, University of Queensland Press, 1983
27 Verlaine: "A Arthur Rimbaud I", *Dédicaces* , *Œuvres poétiques complètes*, ed Y.-G. Le Dantec, Gallimard, Paris 1951, 431
28 Edward J. Ahearn: "Explosions of the Real: Rimbaud's Ecstatic and Political Subversions", *Stanford French Review*, 9, no. 1, Spring 1985
29 James Lawler, 219

> I used to read Rimbaud endlessly, and he saved me from terrible things when I was starting out after Cambridge. I had to do these office jobs, you see, which were not right, they're not right for anybody. I used to complete my office work in the mornings, and I would spend a long time in the pub at lunchtime reading Rimbaud, and seeing the world like this. Which gave me strength to continue. (SS)

Rimbaud – and Redgrove – is, like Orpheus, always descending into Hell and returning. This is the basic journey of the shaman, the fragmentation and rebirth of the self. Redgrove is constantly rebirthing himself, as the artist does, in each work.

This 'descent and return' is a central experience in Redgrove's world. He links it with Isis, Orpheus and Jesus, with the Black Goddess, with the 'underlife' of John Cowper Powys, and with the break-up and reconstitution of the menstrual cycle. More of this later.

The two things – the synæsthetic experience and the prose poem, one of Rimbaud's innovations which Redgrove has often used (in his *Alchemical Journal*) – go hand in hand in Redgrove as in Rimbaud. In a similar fashion, those long, flowing stanzas of Rilke's *Duino Elegies* were an integral part of that revelation which came upon Rilke so suddenly – in the form of the 'terrifying Angel'.

Poetry and Life: The Strangeness of Strangeness

> ...this 'strangeness' is 'strange' because reality is so fucking extraordinary, and strange too because most of us try to live without strangeness, and construct something called the 'ordinary' which never existed. Actually, the strangeness is so ordinary as to be quite natural. The strangeness is wonder and what is wondered at is so wonderful that it is strange we do not wonder more.

Peter Redgrove, letter to the author (5 March 1993)

Redgrove's poetic code is to create poems which describe or actualize this strangeness of living. The strangeness is here, all around us, he says, but we become immune to it. The poet's task is therefore to refresh body and soul, so that the incredible beauty and strangeness of life is once again experienced. The emphasis is on direct experience, not on abstraction or distance. Redgrove hates the synthetic and artificial. Redgrove's poetic ethic is one of direct touches – the Blakean (and Coleridgean) direct contact stemming from the cleansing of the senses. One thinks too of D.H. Lawrence's touch of tenderness, the pure touch, which reactivates hidden/ latent/ unconscious feelings. It is this touch, this new relation, that counts, that reactivates livingness. As Lawrence says: '[b]lossoming means the establishing of a pure, *new* relationship with all the cosmos. This is the state of heaven.' (*Reflections on the Death of a Porcupine*, in *A Selection From Phoenix*, 456-7).

All the wonder of living is all around us. Most of the mystics say this – Meister Eckhart, Rumi, Hui-Neng, Chuang-tzu. Come on, wake up, the mystics say. 'Leap into the boundless and make it your home,' says the great Chuang-tzu, perfectly describing the risk and dare of the artistic act of creation.[30] We are dead, so we must wake up. This is the basic philosophy of any number of artists – André Gide, Henry Miller, Novalis, D.H. Lawrence, John

---
[30] Chuang-tzu: *Basic Writings*, tr Watson, Columbia University Press

Cowper Powys, Anaïs Nin, Arthur Rimbaud. The tragedy arises, says Redgrove, when people don't want to be awoken:

> It's a breakthrough into another mode of consciousness. There is greater understanding than our ordinary waking consciousness permits us. And this, of course, is the tragedy of man, that he doesn't have this, and doesn't want it either. (MR)

The way into the wonder is via the creative processes, the vehicle for the poet being the journal or notebook. Redgrove writes:

> As everybody who keeps any kind of diary knows, it is astonishing how such a practice widens one's awareness. One is astonished at what one loses in the ordinary processes of recollection without benefit of a diary. Themes, thoughts and feelings become visible which the ordinary jerky occasions of daily amnesia would have fragmented and blown away. One discovers continuities of observation which would otherwise have been lost for ever, messages to oneself which would otherwise have been ignored, perhaps something terrifying claiming notice before it decides to emphasize its message with a toothache or migraine, perhaps some subliminal daemon murmuring endearments. The Journal becomes a jungle, inhabited by a whole natural history. Since I have created this jungle, now I must explore it. As I am a writer, I will do this by writing. (WI, 3)

Redgrove's sense of wonder is apparent throughout his poetry. The complete poems printed in this study demonstrate this amazement: 'The Alchemical Honeymoon', 'A Maze Like Us', 'The Pale Brows of Lightning' and 'Falmouth Clouds'. 'The ideal state for ordinary going about' says Redgrove 'is the first stage of orgasmic arousal' (letter to me, 20 April 1994). The poem 'A World' is, like 'Shadow-Silk', one of those passionate and bewildering pieces that is about anything and everything. Like 'Shadow-Silk', 'A World' overflows with life:

> The world full of sugar and rain
> Rubs up against us with its muzzles.
> The hanging lamps of convolvulus
> Shedding scent like radiance, like
> Reading-maps of black light
> That is perfume, the snail
> Fastened to the stem reads its scroll
> From inside, with black light.
> (FE, 57)

In Redgrove poesie, everything is swirled up together. In 'A World', we race from sugar and rain through convolvulus, perfume, snails, wood, clocks, roses, pine-cones, honey, balsam, forests, eyes, etc. The effect is vertiginous and vortiginous, a veritable vortex of words whirled up the poet's shamanic incantations. What does it 'mean'? It 'means' everything, it points towards everything, it 'opens' the reader out to everything.

The poem, like the best of Redgrove's (or anybody's) poems, opens things out. It expands awareness and experience. It is profoundly *interested* in the world. It is a poem that loves the world. In loving the world, the poem sets out to *create a world of its own*. The poem thus becomes a space of its own, the 'magic ring' of Robert Graves, that poetic space that Redgrove calls the 'womb-place', or *temenos*, Merlin's *esplumeor*.

The world is amazing, so the poet sets out to create something that reflects this amazement. The poem is the poet's reflection of the amazing nature of the world. But, as Redgrove argues, the poem itself can be amazing, just as amazing as the world. The poem is thus not a mirror reflecting the experience of old moments, but is an *experience in itself*. The poem becomes part of the world part of the amazing nature of the world.

Take 'Grimmanderson on Tresco', an amazing meltdown of faery tales, mythic imagery, eroticism, landscape, beasts, Christianity and biology, all whirled up together by the force of the poet's sense of being alive:

> A pocket Moonbible by the lacy shore,
> A Ladybible of God the Mother,
> Of ultimogeniture: the lad
> Freshest from the womb inherits
> Nothing but fortune's favour
> And extraordinary companions
> On the electrifying adventure.

Life itself is amazing, this is the point. Life doesn't need way-out fantasies and violent religions and deities to make it astonishing (although these can be fun). As Rilke said, 'existence is magical' (in his *Sonnets to Orpheus*).[31] And Redgrove is fond of saying that 'real life is romantic and ghostly' (quoting G.W. Pabst, the German film director).[32]

Joseph Campbell wrote that '[p]oets are simply those who have made a profession and a lifestyle of being in touch with their bliss' (118). For Campbell, life can – and should – be blissful. That is, one must get into the right relation with life, with the world. He calls it 'following your bliss'. In bliss, the epiphany or radiance shines through, and life becomes full of light . Redgrove speaks of similar experiences. For him, ecstasy usually comes from lovemaking. After lovemaking, reality 'shines', as the mystics might put it. Redgrove speaks of the 'light of the body'. Mystics have their own terms for such experiences – there is the Zen *satori*, the Hindu *samadhi*, the Catholic *unio mystica* or spiritual marriage, while James Joyce spoke of the 'epiphany' of the true æsthetic experience.

Rilke wrote in his *Duino Elegies* of the need to make reality transparent, instead of opaque: the goal is to live in 'the Open'. As Rilke explained in a letter:

---

[31] Rilke: *Sonnets to Orpheus*,,106-7; and see H. Holthusen: *Rilke*, Bowes, 1952; Donald Prater: *A Ringing Glass: The Life of Rainer Maria Rilke*, Oxford University Press, 1986
[32] Redgrove, quoted in Erika Duncan

> In that supreme "open" World, all *exist* – one cannot say "simultaneously", for it is precisely the discontinuation of time which determines their existence. The past plunges everywhere into a deep Being.[33]

To render life 'open' is the goal. Redgrove continually emphasises the importance of promoting/ producing visionary states – the states of post-coital bliss, of daydreaming, of sleep, of poetic trance, and so on. These states are usually relegated to the sidelines of society, but they are not only crucial, claims Redgrove, they are normal. They are the very stuff of life. So Redgrove says:

> Don't daydream, Johnny! Well, of course, daydreaming is exactly what I have to teach my art students. I have to teach them yoganidra, which is daydreaming. To develop it into responsible fantasy. (SS)

Redgrove brings these trance states that are usually ignored into the foreground. He eulogizes the seemingly abnormal. States of consciousness the establishment regards with suspicion as 'strange', 'perverse' or 'wrong', are for Redgrove completely ordinary. But also extraordinary. And useful. These experiences of the 'dark senses' are not imaginary but real. Redgrove writes: '[m]y point is that what one envisions are actualities which play upon our unconscious senses.'[34]

Vision, fantasy, dream are not unreal but part of the imagination. For Redgrove, they are central to experience: 'imagination is the chief therapeutic instrument in Jungian work. And the training of the imagination in a responsible fashion to respond to what is called fantasy, which is visionary eruption from the unconscious or dreamwork, is what goes on when one writes poetry. In other words, it is a process of investigation. We're scientists of the strange, we poets.' (SS)

So the daydream, the artistic trance, the post-coital bliss, is put

---

[33] Rilke: *Briefe aus Muzot, 1921-26*, Insel Verlag, 1937, 333-4
[34] letter to the author, 14 April 1993

to good use in Redgrove's poetics. He advocates, rightly, the creative use of these states which everyone experiences everyday. 'All the magic in his life was rooted in what was natural, and truly magic' muses the hypnotist Pfoundes (SGH, 45). He recommends keeping a dream diary, for instance, so that dreams are integrated into everyday life, instead of being ignored.

Shamanism

What poetry is about is what is commonly called sacred. One can use any number of terms for this sense of the sacramental in existence, that everything that one does is very very real...

Peter Redgrove, *The Hudson Review* (400)

The basis for this poetic experimentation or mode of living is shamanism. The figure of the archaic shaman is the origin of the artist/ poet/ magician/ visionary. The shaman is the daydreamer, the angelic traveller to other worlds, the godmaker, the witch, the medicine man and witch doctor, the 'scientist of the strange', the original magician. As Mircea Eliade writes in the classic work on shamanism:

> As to Orpheus, his myth displays several elements that can be compared to the shamanic ideology and technique. The most significant is, of course, his descent to Hades to bring back the soul of his wife, Eurydice... Orpheus displays other characteristics of a "Great Shaman": his healing art, his love for music and animals, his "charms", his power of divination. Even his character of "culture hero" is not contradiction to the best shamanic tradition – was not the 'first shaman" the messenger sent by God to defend humanity against diseases and to civilize it? A final detail of the Orpheus myth

> is clearly shamanic. Cut off by the bacchantes and thrown into the Gebrus, Orpheus' head floated to Lesbos, singing. It later served as an oracle...[35]

Redgrove is one of these shamanic, Orphic, Dionysian, Pentecostal, fierily lyrical poets (one thinks of Sappho, Shakespeare, Rimbaud, Hölderlin, Keats, Perse). Shamanism features in much of Redgrove's poetry. The shaman can travel to other worlds. The poet does exactly the same thing. 'Poetry's clearly of religion' says Redgrove (Hud, 399). The invisible worlds in religion are utterly 'other' – Heaven is at the top of the World Tree, for instance. For Redgrove, however, the strange, invisible worlds are right here, all around us. 'The other world is this world, only more so' writes Redgrove in 'Other World' (Lab, 10). So the poet descends into life itself, by descending into her/ himself first. In shamanism, there is a deep identification between inner and outer, between private and public, between all realms of experience. This is also the key concept of Western magic, the 'as above, so below' of hermeticism. In 'His Upbringing' Redgrove writes that '[t]he dark world enriches the visible one' (Lab, 58). The shaman is the 'maker', and the Greek *poeitas*, the word for 'poet', means 'maker'. The shaman, like the poet, dreams society's dreams. The shaman is the technician of ecstasy, to use Eliade's term.[36] In an Eliadean mode, Redgrove writes: '[w]e should become technicians of the sacred and study not the abstract ramifications of physics, but the actuality of psychological and biological sciences, remembering of course that any psychology which neglects the inner experience of the woman...is suspect and almost derelict unless we can give our own personal and poetic testimony from actual experience'. (Rim, 177) And again: '[m]en will have to cooperate with the female rhythms for this experience if they want to sustain

---

[35] Mircea Eliade: *Shamanism: Archaic Techniques of Ecstasy*, Princeton University Press, New Jersey, 1972, 391
[36] Eliade, in ib., 1

it.' (letter, 4 March 1994)

The aim is to reactivate the third eye, the pineal gland. Robert Graves spoke of the 'poetic trance', that shamanic state in which the poet creates.[37] For Graves, authentic poems came out of this state – other sorts of 'waking' poems were not the real thing. The Goddess, for Graves, presides over this poetic trance. Every shaman has a different god – indeed, the shaman is her/ his own god, s/he is the god-maker, like the artist.[38] The feminine realm lies behind much of shamanism. Take Shakespeare's major shaman, Prospero: his magic comes from the witch Sycorax. The shaman, like Jesus or Orpheus, descends into Hell, and Hell is of course a feminine realm in Western religion (there is the Mouth of Hell, which is the vagina/ womb, a connection made explicit in much of Western art – in *Troilus and Cressida* or *Romeo and Juliet*, for example). In Redgrove's poetry, too, the male creator takes his energy from the woman/ Goddess: he goes down to her soul-space and brings back his visions.

Rimbaud is the great shamanic poet of modern times. So clearly the shamanic possession took hold of him and wrestled with him. Shamanic possession can be seen as madness, and of course, as Shakey noted, the poet, the lover, the fool and the madman are closely linked. In psychological terms, you can't distinguish between the artist, the genius, the psychotic an the criminal – they share states of obsession and extremity.

Rimbaud said, in his famous 'lettre du voyant' of May 1871, when he 16, that the poet must become a 'seer'.[39] He then proceeded to show us just how astonishing shamanic or 'seer' poetry can be. Any number of Peter Redgrove's poems can be seen as shamanic.

Take the wonderful 'Rainmaking Exercise': a man goes into a

---

[37] Robert Graves: *On English Poetry*, Heinemann, 1922, 19; *The White Goddess*, Faber 1961, 12
[38] Weston La Barre: *The Ghost Dance*, Allen & Unwin, 1972
[39] *Complete Works*, 305-311

wood (a shamanic place, relating to the Cosmic Tree, to sacred groves, to Eleusis, to Merlin's *esplumeor*, to the Druids, etc). The place in the woods is where Merlin, the great shaman of Britain, went towards the end of his life. In their excellent book *The Grail Legend*, Emma Jung and Marie-Louise von Franz retell this stage of the alchemical Merlin myth thus:

> Once again he [Merlin] is captured and in his yearning for the forest loses all joy in life. There is no alternative for his captor but to give in to his longing and release him. However, he allows his sister to provide him with a few comforts. She builds him a house in the forest, with seventy windows and doors, where he can devote himself to his astronomical observations. With her servants, Ganieda settles herself a little way off in order to dwell near him. During the summer, Merlin lives in the open; when the winter cold sets in and he can find nothing to eat, he returns to his observatory where, fortified by his sister with food and drink, "he explores the stars and sings about future happenings." Later he teaches her to prophesy and extols her as his equal. (358-9)

For R.J. Stewart, Merlin's observatory is a symbolic space welding magic and science in the way of ancient Greeks such as Pythagoras:

> The Observatory, with its seventy windows, seventy doors, and seventy scribes is theoretically a very precise and minute apparatus for accurate observation of the night skies, relating directly to the actual astronomical practices in the ancient world, and symbolic to the Elemental and Planetary system of metaphysics which acted as the philosophical and psychological foundation of Western culture. (102)

For Redgrove, Merlin's *esplumeor* may be his observatory, a house of glass, a falcon's moulting place, a shamanic shape-changing space, the place where a pen or plume is used not to fix one reading and leave it at that. Rather, he allows, as all poets do, meanings to come and go as they will. In 'Rainmaking Exercise',

Redgrove plays upon these Arthurian and alchemical allusions, while never, however, letting them overwhelm the poem.

> He finds the centre of the wood
> Where the small switching-house or substation stands,
> The circuit-breakers in their windowless brick
> Creating ozonous ghost; by those transformers
> He considers the golden mud digested by a spring
> At the foot of an ash next to the electrical cottage,
> The witchy tension streaming through the trees
>
> For the thunder builds like an image overhead
> Of its high-tension dwelling here; an ebony fort
> Full of black soldiers piles its battlements,
> A maze in which the lightning flickers.

The images of electricity, for instance, are purely shamanic, for one of the shaman's magical abilities is to be able to control/ conjure fire. The conjuring up of the storm/ thunder/ lightning in Redgrove's poems echoes the acts of magicians and shamans everywhere – one recalls, again, Prospero and Ariel whipping up the storm in the opening of *The Tempest*, or Merlin in the Arthurian romances, while witches during Shakespeare's time, as in any other time, could create storms.

Peter Redgrove: Here Comes the Flood

The Colours of Alchemy

The dark woman in the white coat
With lips red enough to pronounce
Every magical name resounding...

Peter Redgrove, 'Glittering Pharmacy' (FE, 13)

The language of Redgrove's 'Rainmaking Exercise' is shamanic ('witchy', 'wildman', 'magical', etc), and the colours are those of alchemy: black, white, gold. Rimbaud created his notion of the 'alchemy of the word', which is where poetry becomes alchemy, a magical transformative process which can create the Philosopher's Stone out of the stuff of life.

All of life swirls together through the powers of poetic alchemy, the alchemy of poetry, as Redgrove writes in a prose piece, *A Forest of Invisibles*:

> Alchemy is the astrology of earth, and the arts of embalmment and of rending the tomb. Metals are alive like ourselves; the constellations grazing our atmosphere create the fragrance of certain named perfumes; and hence proceed wonders, which are here established. The visible world becomes like a tapestry stirred by stellar perfumes on the winds behind it. A slowworm thrashes on the smooth path; I slide him gently into the grass verge and the green fire which will give him purchase. In the orchard a ginger cat dabs with its sheathed paw at a green apple which is full to the core of gold and black wasps. (CM, 108-9)

Redgrove's poetry is shot through with alchemy and alchemical allusions (see 'The Alchemical Honeymoon', for example). Look at the colours of Redgrove's poems, those blacks, whites and reds which he keeps returning to time and again. These are the colours of alchemy, and of life. In 'The Laborators', title poem of his 1993 collection, he writes: '[w]e laborators wear our coats like snow,/ The black hair, the red lips, the blindingly-pale overalls.'

(Lab, 62) Redgrove is obsessed in particular with black and white. He is always describing white shirts – how he loves white shirts!

> I love white sleeves
> The warm arms in them
> Are like warm sunlight in water
> The lake-lady
> And the mermaid
> Got up for a ball
> You raise your sleeves
> At the brow of the hill
> And the white waves answer you[40]

There's a white shirt in 'Rainmaking Exercise', for example. Look at any of Redgrove's poems and you'll find a plethora of black — white imagery, a mythology of *yin-yang* transformations, the one always transmuting into the other.

White is skin, clothes, lightning, the Moon, clouds, water and glass in Redgrove. Black is the Black Goddess, the unknown/ invisible/ strange/ night/ unconscious/ sixth sense. Red is the colour of life in full bloom – blood, passion, sun, honey, etc. Redgrove constantly spins these three colours together. We are always aware of white lightning in black skies. Or white on white, as in 'Weather':

> An exceedingly white cloud
> shadows across a larger whiter one, a blouse
> Of water folding white on white leans down
>
> As she quits the shop
> Dressed just like that, white on white… (MFT, 5)

Or golden honey – in 'The Case', one of Redgrove's first really good poems, we hear of '[b]lood, cider, rainbow, and the apples still warm after sunset' (SP, 50). That line contains six references to warm or red things. The first part of 'The Comforter'

---

[40] 'One Half of Three Poems Twice', Ark, 236

is a lightning strike of hot/ red/ orange/ honey things:

> The spectrum of all honeys, the sweet rainbow:
> White clover; green honey
> Of sycamore and limetree; acacia of pale gold
>
> And brilliant sun-honey of dandelion; almost black
> Gathered from chestnut and buckwheat;
> The fetid honey of the laurel
>
> Of privet and ragwort too, though to the bees
> It is excellent, they help themselves freely;
> And the thyme and rosemary are ever-thick with bees. (AB, 95)

All this activity based on red imagery relates to the ferment of alchemy. The term 'ferment' is absolutely appropriate here: 'Love makes itself/ By ferment' says Redgrove (Man, 113). Fermentation is a stage in the alchemical process before exaltation, the *rubedo* or reddening. Redgrove says the aim of this fusion of sex and alchemy (the Great Work) in *The Black Goddess* 'is the transformation of human consciousness and its re-adjustment to a more fruitful and feminist path of evolution.' (BG, 141) In 'Tantric Friends', a poem of sex-magic, Redgrove likens love to the fermentation of cider, the body a vat and press. He always uses a naturalistic foundation for the invisible experiences of love:

> Her vat is fermenting my fruit, our tree.
> We are tantric friends. Man is a device
> For harvesting the abundant details of the woman,
> Woman a busy press of the plain juices of the man.
>
> ...What comes is a spirit, a liquor of excited juice.
> The oak vat, and the oak press, the glittering squeezings,
> The tree that ferments the spirit of another tree,
> Friends, tantric friends. The Cider-Master
> Has the knowledge of marriage, friends. (Man, 112-3)

This is West Country sex-magic, Taoist love-magic fuelled by

Somerset cider, where the Love-Master of Taoism is now the Cider-master from Taunton or Hereford. In the Devonshire and Cornish cream tea cosy armchair *Gardener's Question Time/ Antiques Roadshow* world of provincial England, Redgrove injects a fury of alchemical fermentation and erotic transformation.

'One Time' is another one of those short pieces in which Redgrove exalts his lover (like 'Marriage Continued', 'Starlight', 'Kuan-Yin' and 'Cornwall Honeymoon'), just as poets have done since the beginnings of poetry. In 'One Time', Redgrove moves from the fermentation of love to ovens, which speak of the baking of bread, that most wondrous of sensual activities. The erotic mechanics of cooking provide many parallels with the processes of alchemy. It's surprising, perhaps, that Redgrove does not use food more often in his poetry.

> ...Now when I make love the memory of that time
> Rises through my skin, her skin
> Rushes and glistens as it goes, and the black thunderstorm
> Deep in the silent ovens, lightens. (WNP, 18)

Red relates to the blood mysteries of the Feminine in Redgrove's multiverse, which is life itself at its deepest level. Honey, beer, apples, bees, flowers – these golden-hued images are Redgrove specialities. Alchemy distils the aliveness of life: elements such as clouds, bees, insects, water, trees and air embody this teeming aliveness. The bees and wasps are those creatures in tune with the charged-up energies of nature. Despite their short lives (bees spend only ten or so days collecting pollen), insects live fully in tune with the streams of life that so fascinate Redgrove (see poems such as 'Bees and Moss', 'Grimmanderson on Tresco', 'The White, Night-Flying Moths Called Souls', 'Orchard With Wasps', 'Moth on Globe', 'Tapestry Moth', 'Cicada Singing', 'Bees at Chalicewell', 'The Butterfly Essays', 'Wasp-Forest' and 'Guarded By Bees').

One of Redgrove's best prose pieces, "Dance the Putrefact", in *From Every Chink of the Ark*, develops the alchemical process through an extended sequence of dancing and sex:

> I caper with my black lady in the mud. Both lovers are present at the same time, at last. I dance earth and water. The sun dances fire. It reddens the black mud. I am a seed in her red flesh, she pulls me out of the red mud, we are trees laden with red leaves, we are glistening red serpents slithering in the mud. We dance seamless blood-marble with our sour-sweet skins joined. (Ark, 266, CM, 65)

The alchemical allusions here are obvious: to serpents, to transformations, to shedding of skin, to blood, to the sun, etc.

Black and white together clearly define the twin poles of life, the eternal dualities of Western religion, from Zorasterian/ Manicheanism onwards through Christianity to alchemy and Jungian psychology. In alchemy, of course, black and white refer to particular processes, stages in the transmutation of the elements on the journey towards making the Philosopher's Stone, the Holy Grail of alchemists. At the centre of Redgrove's mythopoeia, as at the centre of Powys's philosophy, is a vision of the Grail, firmly equated with the womb:

> I saw with my whole hide of touch. I saw our journey to orgasm (and conception, as it happened, a child made in the rain of blood, a moon-child made at the period) by body-light. I saw her womb with Fallopian wings, and I saw the vessel of life smiling, as it gathered the dead things and gave them life. (SGH, 67)

All these things melt into one in Redgrove's multiverse: poetry/ alchemy/ shamanism/ Chinese sex magic/ yoga/ love. They are all connected, and the poetic experience links them all together. Redgrove's is a unified worldview, a mythopoeia which always tries to unite the multifarious experiences of living.

Deschooling the Senses

Science is common-sense, regimented. We've had enough of that – let us have uncommon sense unleashed.

Peter Redgrove, *Science*, from *the Cyclopean Mistress* (96)

The supergorgeous Arthur Rimbaud, aged 16, wrote: 'the Poet makes himself a seer by a long and gigantic derangement of all the senses. All forms of love, suffering and madness.' (Rimbaud, 307) Redgrove, among others, notes that Rimbaud says a 'rational' derangement of the senses (Redgrove prefers to say 'deschooling'), meaning a systematic/ scientific deschooling, in the manner of the scientific approaches of the so-called 'Naturalist' novelists, such as Zola and Flaubert. Rimbaud's experiment with himself, then, was a rigorous one, not just a dive into decadence and debauchery (although Rimbaud had plenty of that too). Further, Rimbaud had an ambiguous attitude to alcohol and drugs, and the 'Dionysian dance'[41] of his poetry is full of conflict, much of it unresolvable by art.[42] For Redgrove, one of the key aspects of Rimbaud's hallucinations is that they 'present the unreal as real', as Nathaniel Wing puts it.[43]

Redgrove paraphrases Rimbaud thus:

> A poem may be persuading into trance by prosaic but not necessarily metrical skills and at the same time subverting ordinary consciousness from another sense. One will look at a stone, one will describe its shape, and then one will suddenly introduce a notion of its taste. What does a stone taste like? And immediately it's a different stone. And immediately the poetic process begins to operate. When Rimbaud said that what we must have to become seers is a reasoned disorder of the senses, he was talking so much about an upset or an

---
41 Marcel Raymond: *Baudelaire au surréalisme*, Corti, Paris 1963
42 Enid Rhodes Peschel: "Arthur Rimbaud: The Aesthetics of Intoxication", *Yale French Studies*, 50, 1974
43 Nathaniel Wing: *Present Appearances: Aspects of Poetic Structure in Rimbaud's 'Illuminations'*, Romance Monographs 1974

explosion as a synæsthesia: the joining together of all the senses and their mutual illumination thereby. I think you could argue that synæsthesia was the central characteristic of poetry. (PR, 10)

Rimbaud's technique was synæsthesia. That is, the multi-sensory intoxication of poetry, a poetry 'containing everything, smells, sounds, colours' (309). Redgrove calls synæsthesia the 'multi-media show' of life (letter, 20 July 1992). He writes:

> When Rimbaud said that what we must have to become seers in a reasoned disorder of the senses, he was not talking so much about an upset or an explosion as a synæsthesia: the joining together of all the senses and their mutual illumination thereby. I think you argue that synæsthesia was the central characteristic of poetry. (PR, 10)

Rimbaud called it an 'alchemy of the word' and, in his extraordinary *A Season in Hell*, he wrote:

> I like stupid paintings, door panels, stage sets, backdrops for acrobats, signs, popular engravings, old-fashioned literature, church Latin, erotic books with bad spelling, novels of our grandmothers, fairy tales, little books from childhood, old operas, ridiculous refrains, naïve rhythms.[44]

Rimbaud was so hungry for life. He had such a lust for life. He wanted to swallow everything. All at once, whole. Redgrove has a similar appetite. Nothing is too big for him to absorb. Sometimes Redgrove is even more ecstatic than Rimbaud – amazing, but true. In his poems, you'll see ecstasies to rival those of Rimbaud or Rilke. Most of the ecstasies of Redgrove concern sex or nature – and this is borne out by the poems. Like Rimbaud, Redgrove founds his philosophy of poetry firmly on the individual. As Georges Poulet writes:

> For Rimbaud, to feel is to feel *oneself*. As sudden, even as violent, as certain physical contacts may be for him, they are always seen

---
44 from Part II: *Alchemy of the Word, Complete Works*, 193

through a consciousness of self that never loses its lucidity.[45]

At times, Redgrove is more Rimbaudian than Rimbaud himself. Take this stanza from 'The Laundromat as Prayer-Wheel':

> It is the night of the Mystery of White Shapes,
> The angel is here, a splendid presence, like electricity in linen,
> I fold the double sheet up, I wrestle with its wings. (AB, 59)

This is very shamanic, alchemical and Rimbaudian: the angel, for instance, is supremely the shaman in full achievement, or the angel is the Philosopher's Stone or hermaphrodite of alchemy, the transcendent union of male/ female, black/ white, sun/ moon (see *The Alchemical Journal* extract). In Rimbaud, the angel is the 'genie' in that most potent poem of his *Illuminations*. In Redgrove's stanza we also have shamanic fire (electricity), the Rimbaudian commonplace (linen), gnostic duality (black/white imagery), Promethean struggle (wrestling with the wings) and alchemical incubation (night as womb-space for rebirth).

And this is going on all the time in Redgrove's verse. You'll see many images of rebirth, of alchemical transmutation, of shamanic fire, of magical trance. It all seems so extraordinary, but that's Redgrove's main point. It ain't extraordinary at all. All this intense but blissful feeling is quite 'ordinary' *and* extraordinary. It occurs everyday. All you have to do is to come alive, get into the I-Thou relation, as Martin Buber would put it, or get quick with 'Faculty X', as Colin Wilson might say, or 'follow your bliss', as Joseph Campbell says, or come into being, as D.H. Lawrence would say ('[t]o be alive, to be man alive, to be the whole man alive: that is the point' he said),[46] or become a 'seer', as Rimbaud says, or achieve 'deep Being' or buddhahood, as Rilke might say (see his 'Buddha in Glory'), or sink into your 'mythology' or 'life-

---

45 Georges Poulet: *Exploding Poetry/ Baudelaire/ Raimbaud*, tr Francoise Meltzer, University of Chicago Press, Chicago 1984
46 Weston La Barre: *The Ghost Dance*, Allen & Unwin, 1972

illusion' as old Crazy Jack – John Cowper Powys – says. Poetry is a vehicle of achieving livingness, or as Novalis puts it '[p]oetry is the great art of constructing transcendental health... Poetry is generation.' (*Pollen*, 50)

Synaesthesia

> *'A lot of my imagery comes from enthusiastic touch and texture. My skin is very erotic. The books tell me that this is more usual for women. In men, when it exists, the feeling increases with age. I love getting wet, and smearing interesting things on my skin.'*
>
> Peter Redgrove, *The Beekeepers* (16)

The aim, then, of Redgrove's poetry, is to turn life into alchemical gold, to make every moment blissful. The method is poetic synæsthesia. Redgrove cites George Whalley, who says that synæsthesia is 'almost a definition of poetry' (PR, 9). So, for Redgrove, Rimbaudian synæsthesia means 'the joining together of all the senses and their mutual illumination thereby' (PR, 10). Kathleen Raine writes: '[y]et in the final reckoning I do not believe that keener physical sensations are what are most needed to extend the scope of our humanity. Peter Redgrove's awareness in what one might call the vertical dimension of the human spirit does not match the horizontal 'improvement of sensual enjoyment' to which he is so vitally attuned.'

Consequently, Redgrove is a poet who is 'visionary' in all the senses. He constantly focuses on smell, for instance, or touch, rather than sight. There is no poet I can think of with such an acutely developed mythology of scent. Redgrove devotes a section of his major poetic treatise, *The Black Goddess and the Sixth Sense*, to scent, to 'extra-sensuous perception': '[o]dour is scenery, scenery is smell' he writes in 'Fly Buddha' (Mud, 21), and in 'Instead of Ghosts' he describes a '[s]ouk/ Of perfumes' (Tarot, 13). In 'The Good of Her Skin' he writes of 'the good/ Of her skin, never to lose the scent of/ It' (*Abyssophone*, 44). In his poems, scent plays a major role: it is difficult to overstress its importance. In the poem 'In the New Forest' he describes how when it rains a new scent is released amidst the trees:

> As the rain falls on this dust it composes
>
> A mighty odour of forest-soul; I will take some home
> In a match-box, and wet it when I need to return.
> Perfume the sixth state of matter... (FE, 54-55)

The rain composing scents from the earth is not new, perhaps, and neither is the age-old hankering to 'capture' the essence of a place in a box. New in poetry, though, is the notion of smell as the 'sixth state of matter'. In amongst the flow of poetic images Redgrove introduces a scientific idea, using scientific terms. So often Redgrove's poetry is like this, incorporating phrases or passages that seem to be gathered from scientific and medical journals such as *Nature, Scientific American, New Scientist* or the *British Medical Journal*.

In Redgrove, the concept of 'pheromones' is developed poetically. 'Pheromones,' Redgrove explains, are 'external chemical messengers' given off by the body. They are said to communicate profound emotional and physiological effects from person to person.' The poem 'Pheromones' demonstrates what he means:

> The sea hedgehogged in gold,
> Frogged in it, like a great blue blazer:
>
> The great doorman with the labouring heart.
> In this heat your scent is a snapshot,

Peter Redgrove: Here Comes the Flood

Your spoor streams from you like a fragrant picture. (SP, 170)

Other scents include the wonderful perfume of menstruation in the poem 'Starlight', and many other examples. 'Starlight' features that censored image, the blooded tampon (Judy Chicago has produced a close-up of a woman pulling a tampon out of her vagina, entitled *Red Flag*, 1971). In Redgrove's 'Starlight', the movement is from the intimate and private (menstruation and tampons) to the cosmic, the stars. It is the same in Rilke and Shakespeare, this sudden expansion outwards (i.e. inwards) to the stars, the wheeling cosmos, the sudden inrush of heavenly music, the 'music of the spheres' which the astronomer-astrologer-alchemist-shaman can hear with the aid of her/ his astrolabe:

> Her menstruation has a most beautiful
> Smell of warm ripe apples that are red,
> And an odour of chocolate, a touch of poppy,
> And bed-opiums roll from her limbs
> Like the smokes of innumerable addicts between the sheets,
>
> A Morpheus tampon like a tomb of spices,
> Full of spirits, red firework.

There is, for the poet, a deep connection between women and the yoniverse, between domestic space and time and cosmic space and time. The woman menstruates, and the cosmos menstruates ('[m]enstruating, with the stars out').

Peter Redgrove: Here Comes the Flood

The Language of Ecstasy

A new language is needed, as Rimbaud knew, for this new synæsthetic poetry. We see Redgrove stretching for a new vocabulary of scent – in the phrase 'bed-opiums', in the poem 'Starlight', for example, which is so apt, and everyone has smelt them. But we have a poorly developed language of smell. Our visual sense, as Marshal MacLuhan and many others have noted, is well-developed. Hence Redgrove has to employ visual descriptions and metaphors to depict, or hint at, odours, touches and tastes. He speaks of 'the quality of *jouissance* in writing, and the notion that language may be as much a vital plasm as a personality, and that writing is the plasm of the world' (We, 135). So he talks about 'the light of the body' for that glowing feeling after orgasm. Or he transfers scents into visions, or touches into visual imagery. He speaks of 'hearing' perfume, for instance, in *In the Country of the Skin* (17). You have to do this if you can't find the right words to describe something. So in 'Blackthorn Winter', Redgrove writes: '[t]o smell the touch of the wind, to hear the contours.' (UR, 4)

Redgrove's poetry is a mythopoeia of ecstasies, but ecstasies which must be integrated into everyday life. The first great ecstatic poem is 'The Case' (1966). It contains the Redgrovean ecstasy full of heavily sensual experiences, in the three alchemical colours of life:

> And I swam in the thunderstorm in the river of blood, oil and cider,
> And I saw the blue of my recovery open around me in the water
> Blood, cider, rainbow, and the apples still warm after sunset
> Dashed in the cold downpour, and so this mother-world
> Opened around me and I lay in the perfumes after rain out of the river
> Tugging the wet grass, eyes squeezed, straining to the glory,
> The burst of white glory like the whitest cloud rising to the sun.
> …It was the mother-world wet with perfume. It was something about God. (SP, 50)

Peter Redgrove: Here Comes the Flood

Redgrove and Powys

Among novelists, it is John Cowper Powys who has captured most accurately the synæsthetic experiences of life, where so many tiny and seemingly ordinary and inconsequential sensations fuse into illumination. Powys' *Autobiography* is one long record of ecstasies and sensations. Redgrove likes to quote Powys on page 168 of the *Autobiography*. Powys has been out walking and is returning to Cambridge with his walking stick:

> What I am revealing to you now is the deepest and most essential secret of my life. My thoughts were lost in my sensations; and my sensations were of a kind so difficult to describe that I could write a volume upon them and still not really have put them down. But the field-dung upon my boots, the ditch-mud plastered thick, with little bits of dead grass in it, against the turned-up ends of my trousers, the feel of my oak-stick "Sacred" whose every indentation and corrugation and curve I knew as well as those on my hand, the salty taste of half-dried sweat upon my lips, the delicious swollenness of my fingers, the sullen sweet weariness of my legs, the indescribable happiness of my calm, dazed, lulled, wind-drugged, air-drunk spirit, were all, after their kind, a sort of thinking, though of *exactly what*, it would be very hard for me to explain.[47]

You don't seem to find this all-round, multi-sensory description of being alive in Dante, Homer, Shakespeare, Tolstoy or Cervantes. It is such an accurate description of walking. Yet, as Powys says, it doesn't add up to much – he can't say what it all means. That's why such experiences are ignored. Yet they are central to living. This is what Redgrove reactivates in his poesie, these sensations which form 'the deepest and most essential secret of...life', as Powys says. Redgrove has written a poem which features that most Powysian of objects, the walking stick. 'Memory Sticks', from *Dressed As For a Tarot Pack*, combines some of Powys' favourite themes: walking, with a stick, nature sensualism and

---

[47] Powys: *Autobiography*, MacDonald 1967, 168-9

the ambiguous relationship with the father:

> Memory stick, short swagger stick
> Cut from a hedge, abridged
> Walking stick which is the walk's chart,
> He whittles it as he pauses, and leaves the leaf-scar
> Which images the church-tower in the hollow,
> The knot which pictures the duck-pond in its grain.
> (Tar, 38)

John Cowper Powys is an ecstatic writer, who works best when he is moving from one ecstasy to another. It is the same with Peter Redgrove. H W. Fawkner says that Powys is not a 'stream of consciousness' writer, in the manner of James Joyce or Virginia Woolf; rather, he is a 'stream-of-ecstasy' writer (Fawkner, 150). Fawkner write: '[e]verything signifies. The world becomes text, and the reading of that ecstasy... Exterior reality becomes ecstatic reality.' (Fawkner, 152-4) This recalls Redgrove's tenet that '[a]ll surfaces become depths', and that all of life can be blissful, if one becomes opened. 'There is a right emphasis on ecstasy' says Redgrove of my early study of him; 'that is indeed the point' (letter, 7 November 1993). Powys writes in his *In Defence of Sensuality*: '[w]hat this psychic sensuous ecstasy that I am defending really implies is a *direct embrace of life*.'[48]

Powys and Redgrove are right. But in the hustle-bustle of so-called 'modern' living, these sensations get smothered by all kinds of other, seemingly 'important' information. These synæsthetic sensations are dismissed as superficial. Yet, interestingly, Redgrove says that '[a]ll surfaces become depths.'[24] What he means is that all those things you thought were irrelevant and superficial are in fact very relevant and deep. The other superficial things – television, say, or money – are dropped in favour of multi-sensory sensualism. Redgrove explains further:

---

[48] Powys: *In Defence of Sensuality*, Gollancz 1930, 169

> There is a point in sex when you arrive at a different level which is more solid, real and strange than what you were accustomed to. Language can record this...and can induct author and reader back into that state – it leaves the doors open, the surfaces deep.[49]

Redgrove is discussing sex here, but he could be talking about the whole poetic experience. Poetry renders reality 'deep' and 'open', as lovemaking does. The poetic trance is identical with the orgasmic trance. 'Love-making often leads to a creative clarity, and creative work often leads to a deeper love-making' says Redgrove (We, 139). Poetry and love, then, are part of the same magic. The idea is to make the orgasmic state, and the dream state, as creative as the poetic state of trance. All trances interconnect – become one.

This poetic sensualism manifests itself throughout Redgrove's poetry, but it attains its deepest intensity with collections such as *The Apple-Broadcast* (1981), *The Man Named East* (1985) and the later books: *In the Hall of the Saurians* (1987), *The First Earthquake* (1989) and *Under the Reservoir* (1992).

From *In the Country of the Skin* and *Dr Faust's Sea-Spiral Spirit* (1972-3) onwards, Redgrove's poetry became fully synæsthetic: this breakthrough was bound up with Penelope Shuttle's problems with menstruation and the dreams of this time. 'Eventually Penelope's menstrual distress grew much less as she saw how to channel it into something creative' says Redgrove (Met). The dreams feed both Shuttle's and Redgrove's work, and led to *The Wise Wound: Menstruation and Everywoman* (1978).

The two poems from *Dr Faust's Sea-Spiral Spirit* demonstrate as well as any the Rimbaudian sensualism at the heart of Redgrove's mythopoeia: 'Shadow-Silk' and 'The Moon Disposes'. 'Shadow-Silk' is one of those poems that announces real power. It obliterates the poems that came before it by the force of its multiple sensuality:

---

[49] Redgrove, letter to the author, 5 March 1993

> Rapid brothy whispers in the bed.
> It was like silk splitting in me.
> The house is full of the sound of running water.
> A wind blows through the clock.
> It is like a frail leaf-skeleton
> Shivering in a casket.
> We are heels over ears in love.
> ...Our wonder still lingers
> Over the covers
> As within the pages
> All the stars glitter.
> A wind blows through the clock
> And across the garden
> Frothily flows the ghost. (SP, 59, 60)

'Shadow-Silk' is an archetypical Redgrove piece, with its fiercely black/ white imagery, its description of floods and being drenched, its non-stop flow of lines, its incessant rhythm and its urge towards strangeness-in-the-ordinary.

After all, Redgrove doesn't describe weird, perverse occurrences. Everything in his poetry is easily approachable. But he scares critics: he has 'frightened off the critics by writing a great deal and by making demands which were intimidating' writes Michael Hulse. But Redgrove is not 'difficult': his vocabulary, for example, is very simple, refreshingly simple: nothing difficult or arcane here, in his use of words such as *black, flood, shadow, tree, flower, cloud*. He employs simple stanzaic forms – the three-line/ *terza rima* stanza is a favourite (as with Sylvia Plath and Dante). He uses hyphenated terms often, as in the title 'Shadow-Silk', or in 'Frankenstein in the Forest', where he writes of 'Man-skin' (SP, 78), or of 'cursing-lipstick', in 'Four Tall Tales' (*The Weddings at Nether Powers*, 123), or 'Moonbible' in 'Grimm-anderson on Tresco' (*The Apple Broadcast*, 49), and in a stanza from 'Orchard With Wasps' he writes: '[a]pplegenius, loverwasp, scimitar/ Of scented air and sugar-energy' (AB, 55). He has to use hyphenations, because he is constantly searching for the right expression language. Anaïs Nin often used words hyphenated together, moaning that there was no language of sex. It had to be invented, she said, so she had a go. One of my favourite of Redgrove's joined-up term is in the last line of 'Under the Duvet':

Birthwet from its egg of the newborn angel (SP, 189)

'Birthwet' neatly sums up the slippery nature of birth, for birth is all wetness – all that water and blood, as the womb becomes the world, and all the Inside becomes all Outside, where inner womb-space becomes all outer world-space, and a baby is born. The world becomes a 'yoniverse', as he calls it in 'The Yoniversity at Rock' (MFT, 18). In 'Name of Rock of Shells', Redgrove writes:

> I genuflect
> To the moonlit pond, I am running the sound
> Of the rain backwards and getting a fast tape
> Full of voices crying plashy names abruptly
> Enumerating the dead and new born... (WNP, 129)

Redgrove is always doing this in his poetry, running natural sounds backwards to form a new sound, full of voices. In "The Paradise of Storms", one can detect secrets from 'the tree's perfume rising from every leaf' (CM, 81), and in "Excursions" a tree's perfumes create visions: '[t]his sycamore is arrayed with perfumes which enter the world as ideas and visions' (CM, 77). In 'The Wood Tapes', from *The Weddings at Nether Powers*, he writes of an oak tree as being a 'recording of two hundred weather-years,/ The swift clouds, the thunderstorms, the nutrient floods/ Writing on wood', the question being, for us non-trees, us mere humans: '[h]ow do I play back?' (WN, 67). Poetry is thus an answer to the writing of plant and animals and minerals, art answering Nature. The tree absorbs the thunderstorms and winds in its own way: the poet releases her/ his experiential recordings in a different way.

The birth experience is central to Redgrove's mythopoeia – in his poem 'Delivery Hymn' for instance, where the Christ-child is 'warm-shirted in membrane' (SP, 149). Other 'birthwet' poems include 'Condition of Isis', 'Wave-Birth', 'The Visible Baby' and 'Secret Sharer'. So many poems are drenched in the Redgroverse, the Redgrove multiverse. As he says in a poem from *Dr Faust's Sea-Spiral Spirit*, 'Young Women With the Hair of Witches and No Modesty': 'I have always loved water, and praised it' (SP, 62). The clear liquid stuff actually makes things grow, even huge things like trees. As he writes in 'A View of the Waterworks':

What a Waterworks in the seed
To pump the trees so lofted! (*The Working of Water*, 8)

Take this section of 'Living in Falmouth', which is a long poem, much as all of Redgrove's poetry is one long poem. Every line contains a watery reference:

Orion with his brilliant cock shining like the wet spiderweb,
Like a ladder of light heavier than all the world,
Climbing in his drenched plumage like pulsing snow,
Like a silver beaten so long that it gives back light in pulsing juice,
Or like a rainfall so massive it gluts and cannot fall,
Or like a full-rigged black ship, sailing with all knows white,
Or like wet herringbones at the rim of a great black plate... (SP, 132)

The tendency to gush is common in mystics and mystical poets. They are so charged up with energy and experiences, and they have to let it all flood out. So they over-write. They write and write. We see this clearly in writers such as D.H. Lawrence, who gushed madly, or Wordsworth, in his *Prelude*, or in John Cowper Powys, whose *A Glastonbury Romance* is one of the biggest floods in the English language, and, rightly enough, Powys' Glastonbury extravaganza winds up with a gigantic flood that engulfs the New Jerusalem of Albion and leaves everyone seeking sanctuary up on Glastonbury Tor.

So in Redgrove, we find a tendency to gush, to pour, to flood. The sexual connations of flooding aren't lost on him. There is the flood of water at birth, before labour begins, for instance. 'Wave-Birth', from *Dressed As For a Tarot Pack*, invokes the prescient liquids that oil birth:

> The young spiritualist giving birth
> In the spirit of a seance full of sheets,
> Drapes and milky plasms,
>
> Such plasms as will appear, the birth-water
> Moving of itself, the uncanny
> And erotic slime... (Tar, 48)

How odd it would be to have a *dry* birth, a birth and labour without juices, blood, water, mucus, milk, tears, sweat, etc. The wet person is the sexual person: Shakespeare spoke of impotent old men as 'dry', in contrast to Heraclitus and his concept of the 'dry soul'. Redgrove himself lives in Falmouth, surrounded by water – not just the ocean, but also the Carrick Roads estuary system – and this Cornish seascape feeds all his poesie. 'Water is at the heart of Redgrove' comments Michael Hulse. 'Water is my element, the feminine element. Yes, so I think it's urethral contrasted with phallic,' he says (SS). Though 'feminine', uterine and urethral, Redgrove associates water sometimes with phallic energy. He has a phallic god, Orion, who is a celestial version of the earthy gods of ancient times (Pan, Dionysius, Zeus). In the sequence of Orion poems in *The Weddings at Nether Powers*, Redgrove associates Orion with the attributes of Zeus: thunder, lightning and cosmic creation. He also mentions the ithyphallic Cerne Giant in Dorset, who possesses the biggest dick in Europe, perhaps the world:

Peter Redgrove: Here Comes the Flood

> He [Orion] has his photograph in white lines on Cerne Abbas hill
> His stars must have been shrinking there in the enormous dew
> Then the lightning struck, and outlined him
> This is how he ascends at the end of summer,
> He is the lightning that goes up, and the thunder made visible.
> He is a thunderflash, caught on the black ceiling. ('Orion Pacing', WNP, 93)

Redgrove is the only poet I know who has written a poem describing the inner workings of a fountain. A traditional emblem, a fountain, found in Petrarch's eulogies to his beloved Vaucluse landscape, and in many mediæval illuminated manuscripts and enclosed gardens. But in Redgrove's poem, it is the plumbing that fascinates him. Half of Redgrove's poetry sometimes seems to be like one of those 'cut-away' diagrams or plans found in children's books and encyclopaedias. One of his collections, *The Working of Water* (1984) is devoted to the mythology of water and waterworks, reservoirs, flow, dowsing, etc. Redgrove literally drenches his poetry with water. Any number of Redgrove's poems take water as the main subject, from the homages to pubs and drinking ('Legible Hours', 'Alchemical Buveur', 'Buveur's Farewell'), to the poems about bodies and water ('The Moisture-Number', 'Wet Sportswomen', 'Wet Pinup', 'A Dewy Garment'), to the poems about water on a grand scale, either in the sky, in clouds and stars, or in lakes, rivers and oceans ('Under the Reservoir', 'Waterworks as Spiritual Powerhouse', 'Rain on Vaux Hill'). Was it Milton or Henry Miller who said they love everything that flows. Or was it Heraclitus? In 'Woman Bending in a Field' when it rains life itself is unveiled: the veil of rain lifts the veil between us and life: '[w]ater pours down, like life that has suddenly undressed' he writes (*The Apple-Broadcast*, 99).

The poem 'Staines Waterworks' (MFT,41), in, is worth quoting in full, for it is a really dazzling description of the purification of the stuff we drink every day, the stuff we bathe in and suck up into our bodies:

> II
>
> Riverwater gross as gravy is filtered from
> Its coarse detritus at the intake and piped
> To the sedimentation plant like an Egyptian nightmare,
> For it is a hall of twenty pyramids upside-down
> Balanced on their points each holding two hundred and fifty
> Thousand gallons making thus the alchemical sign
> For water and the female triangle.

Water everywhere, the Flood, is a moment of total creativity for Redgrove, as the poem 'The Courtship' illustrates. Rain is not only an orgasm in Redgrove (the 'skin-orgasm'), it also flows on to produce water everywhere, which means creation everywhere:

> Now there comes a quick, heavy shower
> Which I knew springs directly from the moist stars,
> It is the show-er of reflected, hidden depths
> Which clamber down in stairwells all around –
> The clear rain-puddles in their constellations;
> Like statuary you can't see, rainsmell builds
> On these mirror pedestals, and all
> The reflecting hands writing, everywhere. (Lab, 43)

The sea is a 'great sleepy/ Syrup', Redgrove writes in 'The Big Sleep', full of 'Salt honey.../ Ever-living, moving, salt sleep' (IHS, 53). The sea is that dreaming creature that comes ashore and infuses the lives of landlubbers, those people who think they are quite immune from the sea and its effects, as Redgrove writes in 'Round Pylons':

> ...The sheeted sea coming ashore
> And hanging its pictures up in the hedges,
> Its unsalted portraits,
>
> The surface of the sea doubling

Peter Redgrove: Here Comes the Flood

As it opens into sleep,
A source among white sources, cresting. (FE, 36)

What happens in Redgrove's poems, technically, is a tendency towards prose. Some critics dislike the prose-like nature of any poetry, and of Redgrove's poetry. Rimbaud would gush, and often employ the dash – to connect different streams – of experience – which were coming at him – so fast – because of his mystical ecstasies – so the dash allows for the kind of flow appropriate for mysticism. Rimbaud also went for the prose poem, which also allowed for opening out in all directions. Then there is Crazy Jack, John Cowper Powys, the master of the long sentence or *longueur*, as G. Wilson Knight called him.[50] Happily Powys wrote 18-line sentences which flow on and on. Powys, like Redgrove, wants to grab together so many things, so many impressions, so that he often resort to lists, as in the extract from his *Autobiography*, which we have quoted, or in this extract from *Wolf Solent*, where Wolf is on a walk (the archetypal Powysian activity), and he sees the River Lunt flowing

> Past poplars and willows, past muddy ditches and wooden damns, past deserted cow-sheds and old decrepit barges half-drowned in water, past tall hedges of white-flowering blackthorn, past low thick hedges of scarcely-budded hawthorn...[51]

In Redgrove too there is a love of the long sentence, carried on over many stanzas. So that everything in the poem is chained together, and occurs in a continuous present moment, linked by a continuous sense of rhythm and space, an Eternal Now of a single weaving sentence. With no full or stops there are no breaks (a common technique in modern poetry is to dispense with punctuation): the experience of the poem is unified. There are

---

[50] G. Wilson Knight: *The Saturnian Quest: John Cowper Powys*, Harvester Press, Sussex, 1978, and *Neglected Powers*, Routledge & Kegan Paul, 1972
[51] Powys: *Wolf Solent*, Penguin 1964, 150

many sensations or insights in the poem, but, due to the single-sentence structure, they are all melted together. They coalesce in synæsthesia. The poem 'Round Pylons', in *The First Earthquake*, is six three-line stanzas in one sentence (FE, 36), while large sections of the poems are single sentences ('Grimmanderson on Tresco', 'Pheromones', 'Rainmaking Exercise' and 'Four Poems of Love and Transition').

Redgrove does employ strong rhythms, like Ted Hughes, like most mystical utterers. Look at the outpourings of St Teresa, St Bernard or Rumi, and you'll see phrases repeated, slightly altered, but poured forth rhythmically. Redgrove uses rhythm as the shaman uses her/ his drum to beat up ecstasy, just as the poet-smith in the forge of alchemical creativity hammers out art on the anvil.[52] 'Rhythm is present to the entire body,' Redgrove says, 'as both tactile and auditory. Rhythm is of vital importance, yes.' (SS) Redgrove uses very long lines, lines that, as in Walt Whitman, run on and on. Rarely does Redgrove use the pentameter, the blank verse of Shakespeare, or the rugged Anglo-Saxon half-line. In later pieces, Redgrove employs the prose poem – most successfully in *The Alchemical Journal* and *The Cyclopean Mistress*.

Redgrove's poetic technique stems from his method of making poems. He first of all writes in notebooks and collects notes, snippets, observations, experiences, from all manner of sources. He catches lots of 'live things', like children catch newts in jars, and keeps them in a journal (openness, openness, openness is the motto):

> The 'germs' of a work are all about us. The world is full of creative suggestions: it is composed of them. Most of us are too busy in other ways to take up these ideas; the professional creator must be very open to them. They are found in chance observations, words

---

[52] see Graves' *The White Goddess*; and essays on the anvil, harp, hammer and oar of poetry in *Steps*, Cassell, 1958; *The Crowning Privilege*, Penguin 1959; *Poetic Craft and Principle*, Cassell 1967

overheard, sudden headlines, fragments of dreams, the colour of a dress glimpsed through a window. The artist who wants to make the most of his world must set down these hints and guesses, sudden clarifications, brief mysteries, unexpected openings. They are the basis for his sketch-books...found objects for his studio. They are live things, he must catch them on the wing. He must at this stage not worry them to death. He must allow them to reside in his Journal, which is the lobby of his studio, so they can find their own space there, and establish their own presence.

These are then woven into 'second-stage' 'imagery' notebooks. Then comes a prose draft for each poem, then an all-important incubation period, and so on, and on, refining, moving the poems about, changing their form from prose to poetry, until, as in alchemy, some final transformation is hopefully accomplished (see "Work and Incubation"):

There is, then, the germ to be caught, which inflects one with the fever of the work, the active drafting, the conscious experimentation with words and phrases right down to the last comma and vowel; then follows as deliberate a decision to be patient, to lose the work for a time in unknown regions to see how it fares there; and afterwards, to fish it out again, like Dylan Thomas's Long-legged bait, and find in one's nets – what? a pile of bones or a new-born child...

The time of incubation may be the most important part of Redgrove's alchemical process of making poetry, for that's where things happen. The act of creation is crucial, for there one's experiences are set alight – again and again, perhaps. One consciously uses the unconscious, so to speak. Memories, scientists tell us, may actually alter the make-up of the brain cells as things are remembered. It may be that memories are not simply electrical impulses sparking in synapses, but are woven into the very physical fabric of the mind. The deepest, most secret parts of one's being, perhaps, are altered by one's experiences. 'There is strong evidence for the idea that memories are recreated afresh each time we experience them', says Dr Scott Barton, a psychologist at the Ralph H. Johnson Medical Centre in South Carolina (in Jerome Burne). If this is so, then the experience of reading a poem about, say, swimming, may be the same as the experience of swimming itself. This is Redgrove's stance: '[t]he poet is concerned with invoking certain energies in his reader' he says (MR). For him, poetry has a direct, sensual, physical effect. You read a poem about lovemaking, and reading becomes lovemaking. This is Redgrove's version of French feminism's *jouissance*. Love and poetry become one.

Illustrations

Of some places, themes, influences and associations in the poetry of Peter Redgrove.

Skywalkers with immense tension of presence
And extreme visibility and invisibility as well,
The cascades roll past, turn dragonish and then
They are all simple lace very high
On a blue robe which darkens with emergency generating stations
Black as floating mines of coal.

(From 'Falmouth Clouds')

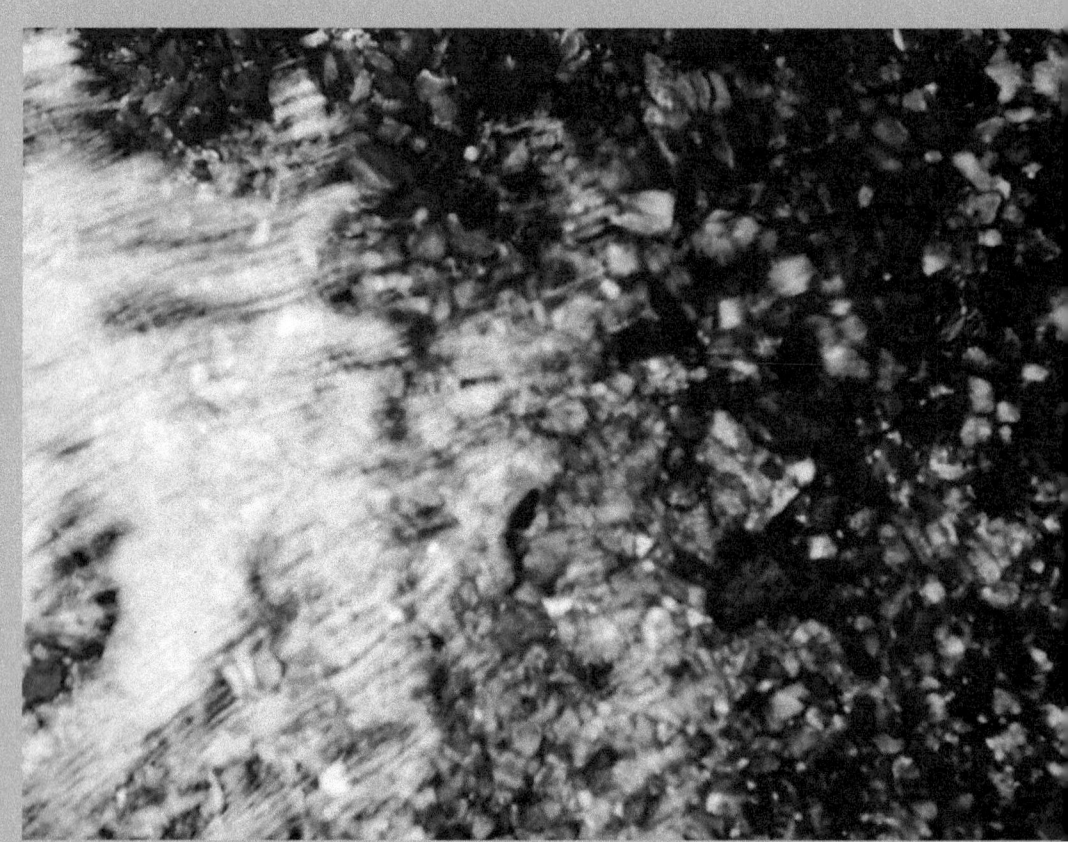

Stream, New Forest, 2004, by Jeremy Mark Robinson

Two views of the Cornwall that features in Peter Redgrove's poetry: the Helford River at Helford Passage, above, and the Lizard at Kynance, below. (Jeremy Robinson, 1993, 1996).

Wheatfields, 2004, by Jeremy Mark Robinson

The greatest possible touch, to bathe.
The wind bathing in the wheat,
The great invisible woman plunges
into the heavy tassels, into the wheat-smell
That is like straw baskets full of new bread;
The wheat splashes round her, it must cry out,
All the stems chafing, like an immense piano plunged into
Which continues playing as she swims…

(From 'Harvest')

The sheeted sea coming ashore
And hanging its pictures up in the hedges,
Its unsalted portraits,

The surface of the sea doubling
As it opens into sleep,
A source among white sources, cresting.

(Peter Redgrove, from 'Round Pylons')

Hokusai school pictures: c. 1830 (above),
woodblock, 19th century (below).

Alchemical texts. Below: Johann Daniel Mylius, *Anatomia auri*, Frankfurt, 1628. Above: *Conjunctio sive Coitus*, *Rosarium philosophorum*, Frankfurt, 1550.

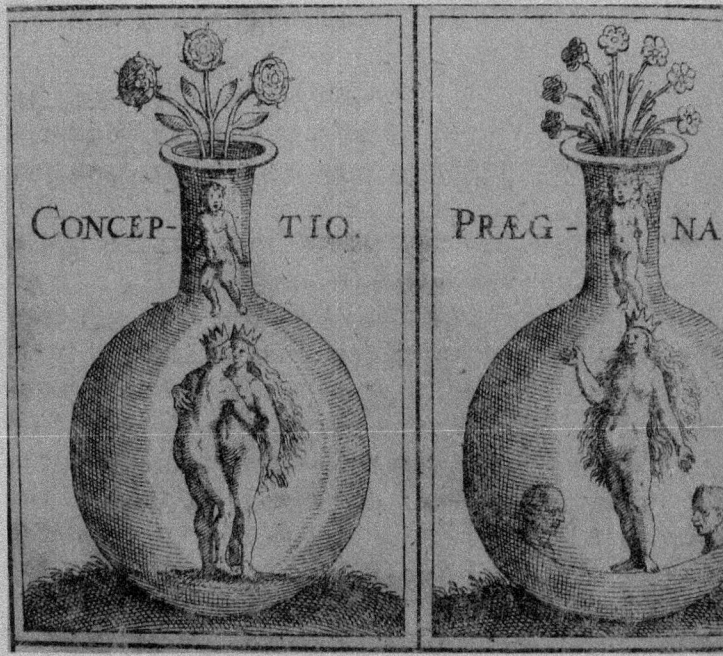

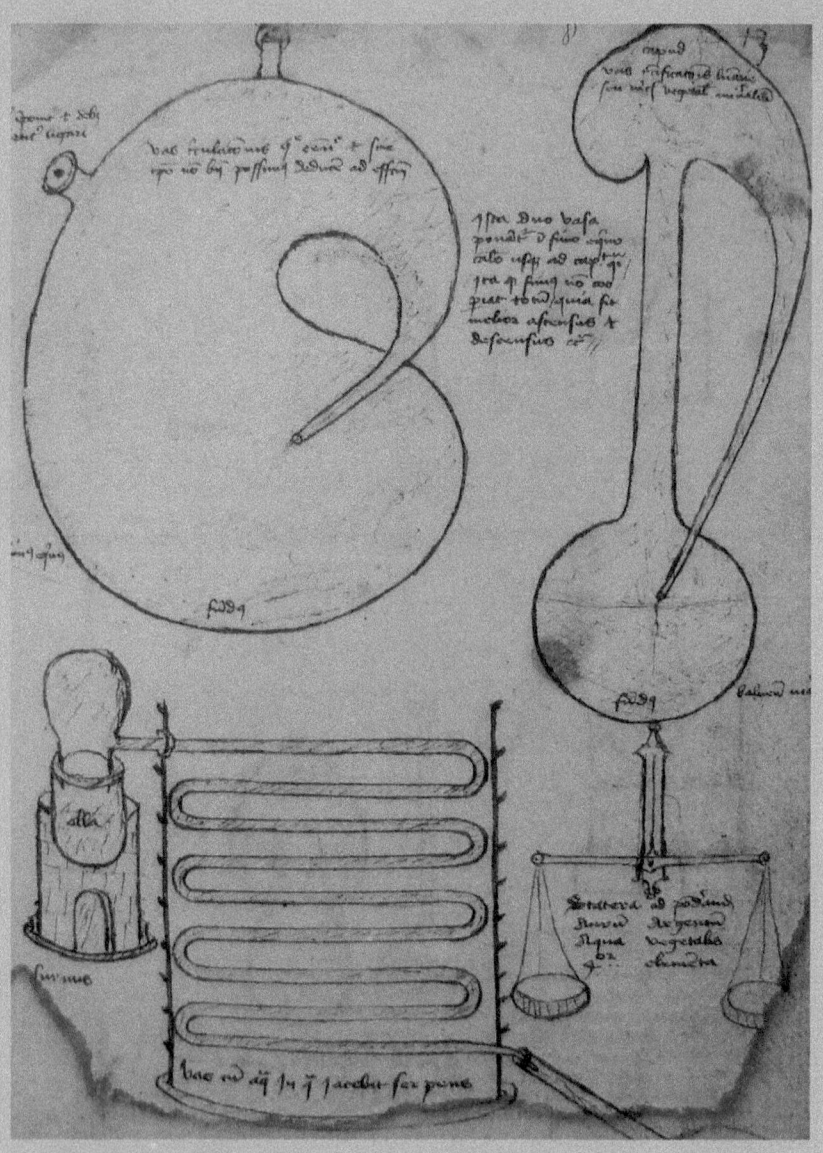

Three

Adventures in the Mother-World: Extra-Sensuous Perception

The bright water unites our skins.

Peter Redgrove, *In the Country of the Skin*, 36

We are surrounded by invisibles, yet we ignore what is invisible, real, potent, natural.

Peter Redgrove, *The Black Goddess*, xvii

…this mother-world
Opened around me

Peter Redgrove, 'The Case', *Selected Poems*, 50

I must connect the skin to the eyes, the eyes to the nose, the nose to the ears, and the tongue to the skin.

Peter Redgrove, *The Sleep of the Great Hypnotist*, 69

Peter Redgrove: Here Comes the Flood

Breakthrough to Innerness

Peter Redgrove has created a science of the strange, a mythology of natural mysteries, a poetry of synæsthetic experiences. Robert Graves produced his *The White Goddess* in 1946, his own 'handbook of poetic myth'; Redgrove answers Graves' book with *The Black Goddess and the Sixth Sense* (1987). Graves would surely approve of Redgrove's evocation of the Goddess in the Welsh landscape:

> The Welsh hills, snow-slopes of hawthorn
> The hawthorn smells of women as we drink,
> The breeze charged with the smell of the Great Mother,
> The Great Woman, the Great Poem...
> (A, 12)

Robert Graves began to write of the Black Goddess, the counterpart of the White Goddess, in the 1960s. In the 60s, Graves wrote more poems than ever before. The new poems are marked by a belief in an ecstatic, timeless experience of love, a transcendent love, a love that is magical and joins lovers praeternaturally over distances.[1]

Graves' new, miraculous form of loving is developed by Redgrove in his book to form a new way of experiencing life – through all the senses, and especially through the 'dark' or 'animal' or 'sixth' sense, that of the Black Goddess, the unknown/ unconscious/ invisible. It is this dark realm of synæsthesia that Redgrove explores in his poetry.

Paul Klee, one of the masters of interiority, put it: '[a]rt does not reproduce the visible; rather, it makes visible.' This is what Redgrove wishes to do in his poetry: to 'make visible'. Max Beckmann, the marvellous German Expressionist painter of those

---

[1] see *Poems About Love*, Cassell 1969; *Mammon and the Black Goddess*, Cassell 1965, particularly the Foreword, where Graves sets out his notion of 'transcendent loving' in a clear, concise fashion

epic, mythic triptychs, spoke of wanting to make the invisible visible, his aim being 'always to get hold of the magic of reality':

> What I want to show in my work is the idea which hides itself behind so-called reality. I am seeking for the bridge which leads from the visible to the invisible, like the famous cabalist who once said: "If you want to get hold of the invisible, you must penetrate as deeply as possible into the visible." My aim is always to get hold of the magic of reality and to transfer this reality into painting – to make the invisible.[2]

This is Redgrove's aim also: whatever is strange, unknown, forgotten, suppressed, he brings into the foreground, into the daylight, and makes it natural. *There must be more to life* – a common enough sentiment. Or as the protagonist of the play in the novel *The Beekeepers* says: '[w]e still want there to be something' (101). 'Ordinary' life can't be all there is, can it? Redgrove says:

> In one's ordinary life, as everyone knows, one sees all sorts of things. One sees in writing, in dreams, in an intonation of somebody's voice, the way they put something down on a table. There are little openings aren't there? I mean in which the ordinary becomes – I won't say miraculous because miraculous sounds like a transcending of the natural state and I think the natural state is miraculous, if one is fortunate enough to be seeing it. (SS)

The unknown is there in the simplest act. Giving someone flowers, for instance, is also an exchanges of invisibles:

> We give each other flowers because
> They are both visibly and invisibly beautiful;
> We give the invisible to the visible,
> The visible to the invisible girl.
> ('The Olfactors', *Abyssophone*, 15)

---

2 Max Beckmann, lecture, 1936, in Hershel B. Chipp, ed: *Theories of Modern Art*, University Of California Press, Los Angeles, 1968, 188

Always there is wonder in Redgrove, as there is in Rimbaud – wonder at ordinary, commonplace things. In 'The Youthful Scientist Remembers' Redgrove writes:

> I am still sober and amazed at the starlight glittering in the mud,
> I am amazed at the stars... (Dr, 18)

Thomas Hardy wrote, at the time of *The Woodlanders*, of this aim to reach the essence underneath reality:

> I want to see the deeper reality underlying the scenic, the expression of what are sometimes called abstract imaginings. (notebook, January 1887)

Hardy looked towards the tragic expressiveness of late Turner for this kind of essence-revealing art. The master of painterly invisibles must surely be Leonardo da Vinci, the most mysterious of all painters. As Paul Valéry wrote of Leonardo in a famous essay: '[h]e feels a desire to picture the invisible wholes of which he has been given some visible parts.' (94)

The innerness or interiority that Leonardo painted is the unknown, dark, nighttime, inner space of poetry, symbolized by the night, by stars, blackness, and infinite spaces. Novalis, one of Redgrove's favourite poets, wrote:

> Toward the Interior goes the arcane way. In us, or nowhere, is the Eternal with its worlds, the past and future...The seat of the world is there, where the inner world and the outer world touch...The inner world is almost more mine than the outer. It is so heartfelt, so private – man is given fullness in that life - it is so native.[3]

Redgrove's philosophy is based on the fact that one can (and should) utilize the energies that lie deep under life. The narrator of *The Beekeepers* wonders about 'a door that would open on another life': of Guy, the protagonist, the narrator says:

---
3 *Pollen and Fragments*, 50-53

...what did most deeply trouble him in his life? Was there anything that seemed archaic and undeveloped, full of energy that was not understood, and must be ridden to be known, like a wild horse? Was there some deep, unresolved irrationality that could be his doorway? (66-67)

The breakthrough for Redgrove came with the poetry of *In the Country of the Skin,* later worked into a novel and a radio play. Redgrove is a poet first and foremost – the other things – essays, novels, plays – are 'cooler', being further away from the 'hot' centre, which is the poems. 'You see, I make my prose fictions from my poems. I make my plays from my poems. And as I described with dreams, the psychological work is also connected with the poetic centre, but it is cooler.' (MR)

What happens is that Redgrove experiences and perceives in a heightened way, the way normally suppressed by contemporary culture, the states of perception called 'altered states of consciousness' in the 60s. These states include dreams, yogic bliss, meditation, the afterglow of orgasm, etc, what 'the Tantrists call the state of the Mother Clear Birth Light' (GH, 11). As he says: '[a]ll of my poetry is really about waking up after sex.'[4]

In *Poetry in the Making,* written for school children, Ted Hughes recommends a basic sort of contemplation to free up one's writing;

> Practice in simple concentration on a small, simple object is the most valuable of all mental exercises. Any object will do. Five minutes at a time is long enough, and if one minute is repeated every lesson, the results will show. The writing exercise follows from this. The pupil takes any small, simple object, and while concentrating on it gives it the treatment described in the Note to Chapter One: full-out descriptive writing, to a set length, in a set time, in a loose verse form. The descriptions will be detailed, scientific in their objectivity and microscopic attentiveness. After some exercises of this sort, the pupil should be encouraged to extend the awareness out from the object in every direction, as widely as possible, keeping the chosen object as the

---

4 in Erika Duncan

centre and anchor of all his statements. Once the pupil has grasped simple electrical connections between the objective reality and some words of his, this exercise, which at first seem dull enough, becomes absorbingly exciting. (63-4)

Many writers can benefit from these simple exercises, even the 'greats' would improve themselves. André Gide used to write into a mirror, the better to study his self. Hughes of course, like one of his main influences, Lawrence, concentrated on particular things, as of his poems show: 'The Thought-Fox' (from *The Hawk in the Rain*), 'Thistles', 'Fern' (from *Wodwo*), 'An Otter', 'Snowdrop', 'Thrushes' (from *Lupercal*), 'Goose' (from *Under the North Star*). These poems directly recall Lawrence's many poems about flowers and animals: 'Snake', 'Bavarian Gentians', 'Swan', 'Sicilian Cyclamens', 'Trees in the Garden'. Painters too hold the observation of natural forms essential and central, usually expressed in drawings. Drawing is central to the art of Leonardo, Degas, Ingres, Kitaj, Klee, Hockney, Rubens, Sarto, etc. Redgrove has his own versions of writing exercises, including 'sealed writing'. The aim of the exercise to open up writing, which in turn may lead to an enrichment of life itself. Redgrove and Hughes have a religious view of art: that is, poetry has a religious or mythic dimension. *Poetry enriches life*. For Ted Hughes, the more you (learn to) write fluidly, the better your writing, and therefore your life, becomes:

> And though it seems strange to say so even life becomes interesting, because one thing that writing teaches most of us is that we are not looking at things as we ought to and we are not understanding them as deeply as we ought. (*Poetry in the Making*, 88)

The aim is to cultivate a state of acute awareness, of right attention to the world, as Oriental mystics put it. Openness, not closure. Awareness, not dullness. Here's an example of what Redgrove is after, from *The Alchemical Journal* (no.7):

...after that to stroke her skin like a cat's so it emits her perfume which combines with mine and fills the whole house with its radiance; and compounds with the radiance and perfume of the flowers, *lumen de lumine*, an electrochemical field, respirable gold, the fruits of the swift tree of life of the lightning, rooted in the sky, blossoming on earth. (CM, 137)

Each Redgrovean subject (bees, clouds, honey, stars, storms) is treated in this enlightened, multi-sensory fashion. But what marks Redgrove's poetry is not so much his subjects – after all, other poets write about skies, for example – but the golden alchemical light he throws around everything, so that things 'shine' with this heightened awareness and mythopoeic openness. Take 'The Brilliance', or 'Visibility Nil', or 'The Alchemical Honeymoon'. Each poem is alive with a multi-sensory awareness, so that a fly crawling over a page can be a fascinating starting-point for a poem, or a drenched white shirt. This is 'The Brilliance', from the 1990 collection *Dressed As For a Tarot Pack*:

> A seething blouse laced with gills is the cause,
> Silvered like a salmon stopping in its own
> Self-stream, a blouse smoother
> Than a fish's belly, yet she
> Is so much of a presence
> He needs no light to see her by; while she
> Has the power of seeing the unseen
> And loving the unnoticed, and her right hand
> Hath holden him up, and her gentleness
> Hath made him great, he claims.
> (Tar, 19)

Like all poets, Redgrove constantly finds intuitive connections between things. Between the perfume of a woman after sex radiating in a room and the smell of a lawn before rain. 'Visibility Nil' is a particularly good depiction of multiple or synæsthetic experience: it is also deeply embedded in an experience of the Cornish landscape. The line that makes it for me is line two: '[a]

telephone box half-full of sand'. It reminds me of a particular old, red phone box at Studland in Dorset, just over the ferry from Sandbanks, which was always half-full of sand:

> A salt-cured house deep in the dunes.
> A telephone box half-full of sand,
> Full of sunlight netted
>
> Like a mayfly's wing, and the sea prowls
> As I dial my number.
> (AB, 57-58)

Redgrove's poem brilliantly captures the feeling of sunlight, of being in sunshine, the feel of the sun's light all over the body. When his poems are not drenched with thunderstorms, they are often sunlit. Few other poets get to grips so dexterously with fundamental but crucial realities such as sun, water, stone, earth, trees and clouds.

For Redgrove, as for me, sand dunes are special places, with their own highly-charged atmosphere. The eroticism of sand dunes is found in fiction, pornography and common parlance, where dunes are places where people go to tup in secret. The walls of sand create a series of erotic spaces, as in Anaïs Nin's story "The Woman in the Dunes". In 'The Poor Man Naps in the Dunes', Redgrove writes:

> I love entering the dunes, which move
> My soul as much as any kind of place – (A, 18)

In *In the Esplumeor: An Alchemical Journal*, a myriad of perceptions are unified by the poet's alchemical pellucidity. Each prose-poem chains together sensations and visions in a single paragraph. Redgrove writes in a similar way to how Julia Kristeva describes Charles Baudelaire's poetry: 'a blossoming of signs... a manipulation of language'.[5] *The Black Goddess and the Sixth Sense* is a poet's handbook, exactly like Robert Graves' *The White Goddess*. Both books are set in a highly concentrated form – like the juice pressed from ripe fruit. Graves and Redgrove collect together all those poetic problems, sensations, ideas, observations and obsessions that have fascinated them for so long. You can dip into *The White Goddess* anywhere, and dredge up something useful. Similarly with *The Black Goddess and the Sixth Sense*, which is intended as a second book in a trilogy about poetry, feminine mysteries, mythology and multi-sensory experiences. The first book was *The Wise Wound*; the third book is, sadly, as yet unpublished, but promises to be the most interesting: *The Menstrual Mandala,* o r *Creative Menstruation* (the current title is *Alchemy For Women*). It's sad that books such as *The Menstrual Mandala* find it so difficult to get published when so much junk pours out of publishing houses every week.

Redgrove in *The Black Goddess and the Sixth Sense* speaks of all-over perception, feeling with the whole skin. He speaks of skin at length – of potentials, currents, electricity, etc (96f). At times, he offers us a recipe for a sensual life. For instance, he writes in *The Beekeepers*: '[o]ver a dinner-table lighted by bees-wax candles, you will find the skin easier, more erotic' (14, also in *Dr Treviles*, 95). This sentence can be a recipe for a dinner party in a style or fashion magazine: 'use beeswax candles to create skin-orgasms all round'.

Redgrove is the poet who has told us what we already knew: that rain is an orgasm:

> The outdoors working in the rain
> In the thundershower leads to
> What we shall call a skin orgasm,
> The whole world turned to glass. (from 'Glassworking', Tar, 9)

---

[5] "Baudelaire, or Infinity, Perfume, and Punk", *Tales*, 321

Peter Redgrove: Here Comes the Flood

The idea of rain as being erotic is nothing new: the ancient agriculturalists of the near East certainly knew – and exalted – the sacred links between women, sexuality, fertility, growth, the seasons and the Earth.[6] So the rain could be seen as the orgasm of the Goddess, a nourishing flood of juice from the womb of the world.

The worst scenario for the Redgrovean poet is to be trapped in a blinkered, claustrophic, narrow perception. This is the scenario, where, for Redgrove, depression is 'withheld knowledge'. To be sensually dead is to be fully dead, and this is the state of many of the early poems in *The Collector, The Nature of Cold Weather, At the White Monument* and *The Force*. These are full of oedipal, domestic and family tensions and pain. The poet/ self/ narrator of the early poems feels trapped, is only partially alive:

> Now I myself am alive only in fragments,
> A piece of uncertain, of filthy tattered weather.
> ('The Widower', SP, 43)

The aspects of death and being only half-alive are marked in Redgrove's early poetry books. 'The sky is dead. The sky is dead. The sky is dead' is the declamatory opening line of 'The Contentment of an Old White Man', from *The Force* (SP, 36). As with Robert Graves, André Gide, Arthur Rimbaud and any number of poets, the home, the domestic relations, the oedipal tensions, are suffocating, something to be escaped, as soon as possible, so that the poet lives a lukewarm, tepid life: 'the beauty and the terror of his life/ Moved him mildly' ('The Collector', SP, 11). André Gide wrote, famously: 'Families, I hate you', while Rimbaud soon took off for Paris in his teens, and had to be fetched back a number of times.

What the early Redgrove poet of the 1960s lacked was a spirit

---

[6] Mircea Eliade: *Ordeal By Labyrinth,* University of Chicago Press, Chicago, 1984; *A History of Religious Ideas,* I, Collins, 1979

guide, a Virgil to pilot him out of Hell, a Eurydice to rescue the drowning Orpheus, an Isis to rejuvenate the dying Osiris. For Redgrove, as for Robert Graves, the rescuer-guide was a creative woman, the Muse. This saviour-Goddess arrives with the breakthrough of Redgrove's books in the early 70s: *In the Country of the Skin, Dr Faust's Sea-Spiral Spirit* and *The Hermaphrodite Album*. But the Goddess-saviour also indicated in Redgrove's first collection of poems, *The Collector* (1959):

> Her silk dress thunders over her head and on to the flounced opening
>   Into quiet
> And her eyes clip open on the ardent oblivion of her resolution and
> The streets and clouds from her high window, swimming and
>   dazzled, rush in.

('Without Eyes', SP, 16-17)

Clouds

Let's start with clouds. Few poets have written so evocatively of clouds. Shelley wrote one of his effulgent poems about clouds ('The Cloud'), and 'Ode to the West Wind' contains a powerful evocation of wind and rain; but, generally in poetry, clouds are mentioned in passing only. Yet how crucial clouds are! Without clouds, how flat and uneventful the sky – and part of life – would be. Without clouds, there wouldn't be sunsets, only a gradual fade down of light. Go out into the open, and immediately you're aware not only of the little things humans make – cars, fences, houses, paths – but the vast clouds, which dominate every sky. Clouds bring rain, and without rain there would be no humans. That's how vital rain is. Rain's far more important than God.

Clouds are wondrous. So it is great to find a poet writing passionately about clouds. And not just about the sight of them, but of their physical properties, their ionization, their electrostatic qualities, etc. For Redgrove, clouds are 'white laboratories/ Equipped with millions of droplet-bottles/ Containing the semiochemicals of the land...' ('The Olfactors', A, 16). Sometimes clouds are dark things that 'radiate dismal feelings', like the cloud over Leeds, or another, at Flushing, Cornwall, where dark clouds were 'a troop of demonic horsemen' crashing into the poet. (GF, 28). Of clouds at Land's-End, Redgrove writes:

> There are shadows and tones in my thought which alter as the clouds alter, but which seem to be sustained also by the drum-beat under my feet. I look at my companion, and she alters too in this glamour, as I realise too that I see more and feel it as a direct consequence of her being present. She glows a little. At least I think she does, but it is difficult to separate this perception (even if I wanted to) from the knowledge that we have a short time ago been making love. I know that this has sensitised us, and we have been re-tuned by orgasm to all that we see and feel now; our skins have an altered pattern of heat and electricity and are differently reacting to one another's reactions, like the amplifications inside that resonant laser-chamber of the cloud, not just on the verbal level or by caress. (BG, 112-3).

In Redgrove's multiverse, clouds are 'ice cathedrals' which resonate over us, and we give back feelings to them. So as the clouds float by, we interact with them – physiologically as well as emotionally. There are poems which describe in passing or as a central feature some great, idiosyncratic cloud. Clouds might seem odd things to write about, really. Perhaps few people bother to look at them anymore. I remember certain clouds, though. An enormous golden cloud sailing over the sea in Dorset in 1985, which I filmed. A soft violet cloud over Richmond Park. Certain individual clouds intrigue Redgrove, such as this one in 'Odour of Magnetism':

> The melon-fresh mud; and here above us, look up!
> Is an old-looking cloud, sparkling fresh,
> An antique flotilla sailing round the world
> Since Drake embarked maybe, a cloud
> That's kept its captain form and steered
> Full of what scents clinging to its blinding sails,
> What magnetics tensing its sunset hull, what sweats
> Of steerage, echoing wall to wall. (Tar, 30)

Clouds also offer Redgrove a multitude of metaphors for love, where clouds are beings with their own life and eroticism; or here, in 'The Olfactors', clouds and rain are the manifestations of love (as the Chinese 'cloudburst' is orgasm):

> For clouds as he walked under day and night
> Gathered night and day inside her like one rain
> Which when he was inside drenched them both. (A, 17)

There are many, many poems to clouds, rain, storms, thunder, lightning and weather working: 'Rain on Vaux Hill', 'Round Pylons', 'Glassmaking', 'Odour of Magnetism', 'A Maze Like Us', 'Air', 'Superstition', 'The Olfactors', 'The Pale Brows of Lightning', 'Whitsunwind', 'Transactions' and 'Cloud-Rustling', to name but a few of the best poems. 'Whitsunwind', from *The Man Named East*, uses the old comparisons of a house as a ship: always in Redgrove, as in Shelley or Shakespeare or most poets, when we're talking about clouds we're also talking about the wind. The wind rising about a house is an ancient experience, familiar whether you live in the Hindu Kush, Chicago or Antartica:

> The aerodynamics of the hold of the house,
> Our wooden, cello-voiced ship,
> Hull of the house, its grip on the wind,
>
> The sheets and rigging of the beds
> As they dream their noisy voyages,

Its heeling in the seaweather... (Man, 71)

'Whitsunwind' evokes Rimbaud's famous 'Le Bateau ivre', that great, incandescent voyage, but also that exquisite moment of yearning at the end of Rimbaud's evocation of his provincial childhood, 'Le Poëtes de sept ans', where the poet rolls around on the canvas, dreaming of travel:

> Et comme il savourait surtout les sombres choses,
> Quand, dans la chambre nue aux persiennes closes,
> Haute et bleue, âcrement prise d'humidité,
> Il lisait son roman sans cesse medité,
> Plein de lourds ciels ocreux et de forêts noyées,
> De fleurs de chair aux bois sidérals déployées,
> Vertige, écroulements, déroutes et pitié!
> – Tandis que se faisait la rumeur du quartier,
> En bas, – seul, et couché sur des pièces de toile
> Ecrue, et pressentant violemment la voile!

> [And as he savoured dark things especially, when, in his bare room with its closed shutters, high and blue, with its arid humidity, he read his novel, always thinking about it, full of heavy ochre skies and drowning forests, of flowers of flesh strewn in starry woods, vertigo, crumblings, disaster and pity! – while the noise of the neighbourhood continued down below, – alone, and lying on pieces of canvas, and violently envisioning an unbleached sail.][7]

The cloud-sensibility is nothing new in Redgrove – one of his earliest collections, *The Nature of Cold Weather*, contains poems about mist, for example. The electricity and energy of storms informs so much of Redgrove's poetic outlook. It is the energy of life itself, whether one calls it 'the Moon', or 'the Goddess', or 'God' or 'Tao', or whatever. Look at the wonderful 'A Maze Like Us', which speaks of 'serpent-lightning streaks, the fire-snake' (IHS, 31):

---

7 *Complete Works*, 78, translation: author

Peter Redgrove: Here Comes the Flood

> The lightning zig-zags through its maze.
> The thunderbird takes feathers of blue flame,
> Flaps immense shadows in his mountain aviary
> Of clouds, immense lightnings
> Among the heaped water, the heavenly
> Cisterns with their gunpowder disposition
> That are in this moment sapphire,
>
> This moment, ebony scented with electricity.
> There is a darkness that reveals other lights
> Present in this thunderstorm, present in the mother
> Of clouds. I switch on the electric fan
> In the sultry heat and the air is
> Folded, escaping billows of ether.

Storms of course are fantastic sensual experiences, veritable orgasmic 'skin orgasms'. Redgrove devotes many pages of his *The Black Goddess* to storms, maintaining that storms can be very creative (BG, 78f). In 'A Dewy Garment' Redgrove speaks of 'the film a black-and-white thunderstorm/ Flashing eighteen times a second' (IHS, 27). One imagines that Redgrove would adore the American artist Walter de Maria's *Lightning Field*, which is a grid of steel poles, each two inches in diameter, 18 feet high, 30 feet apart from each other, set in five rows of seven in the Arizona desert. De Maria's piece of land art actually attracts lightning, and the photos of the lightning strikes are very impressive.

Redgrove has created his own piece of land art which attracts lightning: the poem 'The Pale Brows of Lightning':

> And lightning opens its shutter but an instant,
> When it catches you burn like a candle,
> What is that lambent shadow fluttering into the woods
> In its own blue light that illuminates primrose
> The ripped tree's flesh?
>
> It is time, but will he recall lightning
> Or the clouds of shame merely, that gather?
> It is her discipline not to permit them

> And with a differing kiss she clarifies him
> Being full of his lightning and his sitz.
> (Man, 80-82)

Storms are highly erotic, and when Redgrove is writing of a storm in a poem he is also writing of the feminine mysteries, of the Goddess, sometimes embodied in dragons with their snake-like lightning strikes. In one memorable image, thunderstorms are likened to rampaging lions:

> Burning the images
>
> Of winter, rolling the fires down the hill
> On St John's Day, the thunderstorms
> Ramping like lions around
>
> The circus of the horizon...
> ('The Drumming Stars', Man, 36-37)

Robert Graves would approve of the mythic aspects evoked here – Midsummer, fire, St John and lions – for one of the most startling of Graves' many images of the White Goddess is when she is riding a lion. In another poem, a thunderstorm is 'like a lion's head' ('The Passengers', in *Dr Faust's Sea-Spiral Spirit*, 15).

For him, the 'whole-body' sensation of the weather is linked to the orgasmic state. So one often finds women in storms in his poems, or wet garments, which also point towards a charged eroticism. One finds the eroticism of nature in most nature mysticism and poetry – in Wordsworth, Goethe, Coleridge, Heine, Shakespeare, Rilke. For Redgrove, the body is a weather system in itself, as is a house: '[f]amilies create living vessels of alchemy in their homes, distilling human weather from room to room' he writes (BG, 68). In 'Far Star' he employs those familiar Redgrovean metaphors; a woman as a broadcaster, a house as a transistor, the feelings of the family like weather:

> It is like living in a transistor with all this radio
> Which is the inner weather of the house
> Presided over by housegoddesses who turn
> Everything that happens into perfume and electricity;
> Oh! she cries, what a blessing – and I smell the blessing
> Like a candle lighted, a scented flame that spreads
> Through closed doors, opening them... (IHS, 36)

Redgrove's point is that there is a scientific, physiological basis for such commonplace notions such as the 'atmosphere' of a room, or the way the weather affects us. Cornwall features prominently in Redgrove's mythology of weather and the 'skin orgasm', because the weather is so changeable in Falmouth (BG, xi), and the nearby Lizard peninsula creates weather, he says in 'Weather Begins Here (Cornwall)':

> Much of the weather of England is born on Goonhilly Down,
> It is dispensed from there in concentrated form
> That England dilutes *ad lib*. Sometimes syrup-of-thunder
> With streaks of lightning in it, or solid sunshine
> Hewn in convenient lengths for up-country... (AB, 12)

Redgrove sees himself as living in a series of interconnecting alchemical vessels. First there is the alchemical womb of his lover; then the vessel of her body, in which every tumultuous change, or delicate change, in the weather of the cosmos occurs; then there is the alchemical vessel of the house, which is a laboratory with many interconnected rooms; then there is Falmouth; then Cornwall; then the sea; then the whole universe. Lastly, and importantly, there is the chemical/ alchymical vessel of his poetry, in which every other alchemical vessel is joined together by magical correspondences and dream visions.

'Falmouth Clouds' is typical of Redgrove's vision of the whole world as an alchemical vessel, full of a mass of energies, experiences and transformations which are all part of the same continuum, whether they be kisses, trees, clouds, memories, ideas, orgasms or bees ('[b]ees are important' says the poet Guy in *The Beekeepers*, 12):

> I
>
> The weather, opening and closing
> Doors in the head.
>
> Opening them gently like
> A gradual suffusion of sun, or
> Slamming thunder-splattered doors shut.
>
> VI
>
> An exploding herb-garden or laboratory
> Shoots across the sky,
> Arrests one's head and simultaneously
> Across the inside of that dome
> Plants horticultures of changeable perfumes.
> (UR, 15-17)

Redgrove is always talking about magical spaces, the laboratory, *temenos*, womb, moon-place, Merlin's 'esplumeor' (a term that fascinated Powys' John Geard in *A Glastonbury Romance*). Robert Graves spoke of the poem as creating a 'magic ring' around the reader.[8] Each poem is a magic circle, a womb-place where transformations can occur. For Redgrove, a poem must create experiences as well as 'record' or 'describe' them. This notion of feedback works on a physiological as well as psychic level (these ideas are discussed in *The Wise Wound*). In a piece on *The Apple-Broadcast*, Redgrove explains this notion of the poem giving back something:

> It is currently held that a poem must arise out of experience. True enough, but only half the story. A poem must also *give* you an experience...The poem is a tuning or feedback device which alters or adjusts our capacity to respond to the world. ("On *The Apple-*

---

8 Graves: "The White Goddess", lecture, 1957, in *Steps*, op.cit., 96

Broadcast", 166-7)

Responding to Donald Davie's *Articulate Energy*, Redgrove says:

> My pleasure expands and takes various forms within the poem. That's the first sensation, and it's the thing I want in my own poems... it's as though the sentence is a space which is filled with dynamic energies which either hold still or interact... As though there was in the poem an articulate energy (Donald Davie's words) transmitting itself from sentence to sentence and from part of the sentence to another in various ways. Causing various pressures and lightenings and darkenings as it does so. – It's a very material, physical thing. (Hud, 393)

We do more than intellectually digest a poem when we 'read' it. Cultural/ postmodernist theory has demonstrated how crucial 'reading' is. Reading becomes writing: one 'writes' one's own texts as one interacts with texts. One 're-writes' 'Shakespeare' as one 'reads' the plays or poems. Redgrove is arguing for a physiological foundation for this feedback, terming it biofeedback. In the poetic experience, in reading or hearing or writing poetry, all manner of physiological events are happening:

> If you record blood pressure, skin resistance, pulse rate and this kind of thing, when people are listening to poetry, you can persuade them to do it... you find that there are profound changes. You can do it on the E.E.G., that's the electro-encephalogram, the brain waves, this is sometimes done, but it's much better to do on the skin, which is covered all the time by a kind of rainbow of electrical patterns, which run over the skin and seem to bypass what we call our conscious minds. If a person is reading poetry or having poetry read to them... the results are this – they may be paying very little attention or they may give very little account of this in their conscious minds, but the body becomes alive with, if you like, the colour of the poem. It's a very extraordinary and beautiful thing, that. I think we are very used to repressing this kind of event. If we relax of course we can feel into our skins and our emotions much more deeply, and poetry is providing a induction into this deeper life, without a doubt. (PR, 6)

Painters know about these things, of course, when they chose particular colours. It is well-known, for example, that the colour orange increases heartbeat and raises blood pressure.[9] And linguists know that the mouth and vocal cords move when people 'speak' aloud in their minds – their bodies react to words, physically.[10] And everyone knows there are different levels of speaking: silently, in the head, or aloud, in the head, or with the voice. And when you add the spoken voice to poetry, it becomes really extraordinary:

> When we are speaking we are altering the feelings in our body through circulation and respiration; we are taking thought of our speech, we are engaging in a kind of inner dialogue with our physical capabilities. Poetry has to be spoken, *is* spoken; even when you appear to be reading silently there is a voice going on. I'm thinking of the heroic couplet – the Augustan heroic couplet is a most bracing measure, one feels braced by it as by a walk in a stiff breeze. It's physiological. (PR, 7)

Redgrove has a poem about this: 'The Girl Reading My Poetry' (in *In the Hall of the Saurians*), where the smells given off by the reader and audience affect the poetry reading in invisible but tangible ways:

> And she stands there spattered with it
> And glowing with the fine smell,
> And takes her smiling breath
> Of the cloud of quelques fleurs and cordite
> And drinks up these chemicals and the electricity
> Generated by applause inside the invisible
> Air-hued cloud of alchemy
> And imagery poetry-gas. (IHS, 30)

---

9 see Jeremy Robinson: *Glorification: Religious Abstraction in Renaissance and 20th Century Painting*, Crescent Moon 1990; Maurice Tuchman: *The Spiritual in Art: Abstract Painting 1880-1985*, Los Angeles County Museum of Art, 1986
10 see Benjamin Walker: *Body Magic*, Granada 1979

Mud

When I sat you down in the mud in your white dress, you said it made you feel like a goddess.

Peter Redgrove, *In the Country of the Skin* (7)

Do you want to get wet? A good way of achieving total, sensual immersion in the pulsating natural world is to dive and dance in mud. One achieves 'the complete relaxation' writes Redgrove in 'Mudlark' (Mud, 26). Like clouds and rain, mud is one of Redgrove's main interests. Redgrove writes at length about mud: there is the sequence "Dance the Putrefact", the book *The Mudlark Poems*, and many others poems about mudbathing. If you're going mud larking, dress properly: a crisp white shirt is *de rigeur*. The whiter the better, the more spotless the clothes the greater the contrasts with the 'black metal mirror' ('Advanced Mudlark', Mud, 22). It's a flip from purity to a different kind of purity, from white to black in a way that goes beyond Manichaean dualism. In "Mudlark Instructions", a prose poem, Redgrove writes:

> A person whose lights are not lit may acquire an ambiguous phosphorescence by rolling in mud. Approach the sludge lagoons at dusk through silver birch, your heart in your mouth, your clean clothes rustling. Teeter on the turf brink facing the array of calm black mirrors which are directed at the sky to absorb all rays from the cosmos and to precipitate them as itself, for that is why they are black. Had your microscope-equipment you would understand that you are standing in front of a great laboratory lying on its back. This laboratory throngs with the ghosts of trees, which are being treated with both electricity and perfume by an indigenous workforce. You are about to become that laboratory. (CM, 47)

In mud-dancing, the body becomes swathed in blackness: the activity of mud-larking is thus a vivid expression of getting in touch with the unknown. The unknown or the invisible is black in traditional symbolism, so in mud-bathing one becomes wholly dark, one is clothed in the unknown. The journey from white to black is an occult transformation, like Orpheus' descent into the Underworld. It's a journey which resonates in witchcraft, where, as in the Eleusian mysteries, initiates have to get used to utter darkness. As Redgrove writes in 'Mudlark VI':

> Our young folk
> Before they enter the craft, wear white; then one day
> Their skins full with invisible colours,
> They yearn for all knowledge and run wild
> Rolling in the yeast marsh to learn the stains
> of all the plants at once... (Mud, 18)

The skin is opened, becomes acute in its perceptions. The revitalization of the skin is the outward manifestation of an inner rebirth. To fall into that lake of dark mud is verily a return to the womb. The 'return' is not a return, a going back, a regression, but really a reconnection with Nature, which is the original womb, the earth-womb, the Earth Mother. The 'return' is the realization of one's own nature and one's relation to Nature. These are the relations that modern urban life seems to obscure. 'I want to dream awake, and dream as I am touched, and as I touch' says Pfoundes in *The Sleep of the Great Hypnotist* (68). Mud-bathing, for Redgrove, is a renewal of that direct, synæsthetic touch with the world. For every sense, not just touch, is re-activated in mud-bathing. In 'The First Mudlark', Redgrove writes:

> I am body-masked in bacteria and volatilities
> And fellow-drinkers, the bacilli are delighted,
> They swarm celebrating over Gulliver,
> They throw him down again in unction;
> It is our fertility-dance, I rise in black.
> (Mud, 9)

Even if you're not submerging yourself ritually in mud, the

invisible water is right under your feet: everywhere you walk there are underground streams and lakes. 'Water has very marvellous qualities' (*The Glass Cottage*, 45). There are layers of water right under you now, in your house, under your street, and in the forest:

> There is a moon of water under the forest,
> A water-table in which the moon's gravity
> Shines invisibly...
> ('Water-Table', *Abyssophone*, 21)

Total Body

Every beloved object is the focus of a paradise...One touches heaven, when one touches a human body.

Novalis, *Pollen* (30, 59)

Redgrove argues for all the neglected senses. 'We must look for what is neglected in genteel life' he says (Rim, 177). He writes: 'our eyes see the rain, but our whole bodies feel it is raining – it touches us, its music sounds on roads and buildings' (BG, 92). In one extraordinary image, from 'Success', the narrator and his lover have 'a shower in perfect darkness' (MFT, 16). Here, in this single image of taking a shower in total darkness, we find Redgrove's usual concerns: a 'total body experience', here involving water, of course, the shower echoing the mudbath; the darkness has the usual Redgrovean connotations of alchemy, with the shower stall acting as an alchemical vessel; and erotic togetherness.

What happens in Redgrove's poesie stems largely from the

post-orgasmic state: he and his lover go out walking after lovemaking, and the world is perceived in a fresh way, as if after a storm, the air lucid, the perfumes of the world newly intoxicating. Redgrove says: '[w]e find that if we go to bed at night, make love, dream, and sit down for breakfast the next morning, there erupts an amazing firework in life: the senses have been cleaned, the world transformed.' (Met)

The juices and essences of orgasm, exchanged by the lovers and studied by Taoist 'Love Masters', become the rainfilled streets and the clouds above. The weather of the bodies conjoined in orgasm becomes the weather of the whole house and, by extension, because poetic magic is all-inclusive, the whole world. See the essences being exchanged in 'Cornwall Honeymoon', a poem which is as much about the Cornish landscape as it is about love and eroticism. Indeed, these things are the same: the landscape, the lovescape, the sexscape. One can speak of the 'landscapes of love' in Peter Redgrove, for his landscapes are filled with erotic feeling, as 'Cornwall Honeymoon' shows powerfully:

> Kaolin. A white shadow
> Spread across half a county. All the streams
> Flaming white. The soil packed
>
> Underfoot solid with light. A beach
> With drifts of dead leaves instead of pebbles.
> Flowering fogs and the cold fur of moths.
> (SP, 190)

The imagery fuses: light, storms, stars, oceans, black/ white, water, glass, clothes, etc. Thomas Hardy would say that he walked to his beloved to see her, but Redgrove changes this: "I *rainwalked* to Annalee in Lower Lodestone' ('Annalee and Her Sister, *The Laborators*, 46 [my italics]). The term 'rainwalked' changes the sense of walking entirely. It becomes a Powysian walk, where walking is a series of ecstasies. (There is a clue, too, in that placename, 'Lower Lodestone' – the word 'lower' refers, as in 'nether' of 'Nether Powers', to the erotic, dark underlife of things).

And, wait a minute, there are stones that are full of light in 'Cornwall Honeymoon': '[t]he soil packed/ Underfoot solid with light'. In Redgrove, the landscape itself shines. It is radiant. For Lawrence Durrell the magnetic light of Greece comes out of the rocks. Durrell wrote of walking on 'miracle ground'. It is the same in Redgrove: stones shine, they are full of liquid, like dragon's eggs. In Redgrove, stones are not dead, they are alive. In 'The Ninety-Two Demons', Redgrove describes a man rockpooling in a world of violet light like that of Greece:

>   iodine harvest, the violet element,
> Evening element of the violet clouds vast as the shallows,
> Vast languid harvest beating in the rock-pools. (WNP, 97)

The sculptor Brancusi recognized that the egg-shape is a cosmic shape, encompassing all of space and time, like the tree. In Tantrism, we hear of the World Egg (Rawson, 195), which is connected to the phallic spirit, energy and symbol of Indian religion, the lingam. The phallus or lingam, one of the great icons of Indian religion, is often depicted as an egg (the Egg of Brahman or Svayambhu). In Redgrove we find similar connections to those made in Tantrism between eggs, phalluses, creation, sexuality and birth. So when light shines out of stones in Redgrove's 'mother-world' (his poetic world), it signifies, again, the creative nature of everyday experience. Stones, they lie about the world everywhere. They are seemingly very ordinary. But in Redgrove's alchemical world, stones are full of light and life. The poetic connections, between stone, phallus, light (male creative fire), creation, liquid (semen), etc, seem to be distinctly masculine, but Redgrove's stones, like the Indian egg-shaped lingams, are also wombs. In poems such as 'Stonelight, Moonlight, Stonelight (Scillies)', Redgrove evokes a yoniverse of creative energies flowing from storms to water to cliffs to cloud to grass to light to the sea. It is a cosmology of creative, erotic poetry. The sea is that manifestation of the cosmic force that powers everything. But, whether the sea is the cause or effect, like the stars, of life, it is crucial to Redgrove's poetry, which is all embodied by and powered by the sea:

> ...The water becomes black and will not send back any images.
>
> A star touches the water, the whole sea
> Becomes a cog of tines, a clock of dancing cogs, then the faint-gold
> Touch of the star goes and the sea
> Is a restless liquid full of self-lighted stones. (IHS, 48-49)

In Thomas Hardy, nature mysticism is of the traditional kind: Gabriel Oak under the wheeling stars in *Far From the Madding Crowd*; Tess in the ethereal dawns of Talbothays; in *The Woodlanders* Giles Winterbourne has a sacred relation with the trees; and in so many poems the Hardyan suitor wanders over the Dorsetshire hills to see his betrothed so many times, pausing at every graveyard along the way to scrutinize the tombstones. All this nature poetry is familiar. It is the standard English response to Nature, found in Wordsworth, Shelley, Shakespeare, Spenser, Donne, etc. But in Redgrove – and in Powys, Rilke, Perse, Novalis, Rimbaud and others – sensuality is of a different order. In Redgrove, the Judaeo-Christian God is not found in the workings of the universe – there is no Prime Mover, or whatever, as in Hardy or Wordsworth. There is, simply, the incredible, intoxicating reality of the thing-in-itself (something Rilke and the Existentialist philosophers such as Heidegger and Sartre tried to get at when they spoke of *innigkeit*, or is-ness, or 'thereness', as Zen Buddhists might say). For Redgrove, 'God' is the thereness of the world, identical with the beingness of the philosophers. As he writes in "Philosopher and Skin": 'reading, he understood that [as with T.F. Powys] God was the ground of being: 'The ground. That's it! God is the ground!' looking out at the trees, and at the fresh rain soaking into God.' (CM, 117)

For poets, the thing-in-itself, the thereness of the world, must be primary. So the cloud is *there*. The tree. The apple. The ocean. So a rain shower can be a 'skin orgasm' or, in 'Living in Falmouth', a fall of dreams:

> Clouds-dreams let loose a moment of shower,
> Dream-tides knock the fencing dream-boats
> And two-legged dreams make one flesh. (SP, 127)

Sex, Weather, Clothes, Body

It's clear by now that Peter Redgrove's relation with the world is erotic. The weather is erotic; Nature is erotic; and poetry streams from the orgasmic state. So Redgrove will speak of the sexuality of the weather, and the meteorological quality of sex (while feminists and cultural theorists speak of 'the sexuality of texts' and 'the textuality of sex').[11] The world is flowing and buzzing with streams and drones of energy which Redgrove turns into texts and poetry. Like an aerial angled out into the darkness of the ether, Redgrove captures these streams of life which are being broadcast 24 hours a day and, via the invisible and arcane electromagnetic processes of poetry, he sets them down in words. 'Invisible rays tumble over the hills and through the hills like a

---

[11] see Toril Moi: *Sexual/ Textual Politics: Feminist Literary Criticism*, Methuen 1985, and Mary Eagleton, ed: *Feminist Literary Criticism*, Longman 1991

stiff breeze of watered silk that we cannot see' he writes in "My Shirt of Small Checks" (CM, 19), one of the many pieces that employ the broadcasting metaphor or similitude. The energies of life are being broadcast all the time' the trick is to pick them, using extra-sensuous powers and incorporate them into one's own life. Redgrove cites Coleridge often as a weather-soaked poet. Robert Graves refers to Coleridge as a Muse-poet, and quotes him in *The White Goddess*. Redgrove refers in an interview to Coleridge's 'Dejection: An Ode': '[i]f you look at Coleridge's Dejection Ode, you see that it's almost the weather speaking those thoughts, it's the weather which solves the problem of his depression.' (PR, 8) In Coleridge's 'Dejection' we can see that visionary, elemental, Nature-soaked energy which is so much a part of Redgrove's poetry. The notion of Nature as a garment or shroud which envelops humanity also chimes with Redgrove's vision. This is from Coleridge's poem:

> O Lady! we receive but what we give,
> And in our life alone does Nature live:
> Ours is her wedding garment, ours her shroud!
>   And would we aught behold, of higher worth,
> Than that inanimate cold world allowed
> To the poor loveless ever-anxious crowd,
>   Ah! from the soul itself must issue forth
> A light, a glory, a fair luminous cloud
>   Enveloping the Earth –
> And from the soul itself must there be sent
>   A sweet and potent voice, of its own birth,
> Of all sweet sounds the life and element!

The direct experience Redgrove has with the world has an 'erotic' dimension to it; Catholics might call it 'spiritual' or 'Godly'; Buddhists talk about becoming 'self-luminous'; for Taoists, to be in tune, so to speak, with the world is to 'follow the Tao', and vice versa. For Redgrove, all these terms speak of the same magical, spiritual, sexual, natural, ordinary and extraordinary experience. As Redgrove knows, you don't have to mention pricks and clits and endless tupping to be erotic in writing. This is from *Everything They Tell Him Is True*:

> The forest jumping with particles of light distilled in water. The brook deep in the forest, one of the moon's ravelling sleeves. Cuff of moon, dark shirt of water. The forest by the sea, the docks among the tall senior trunks. Sun-thatched thunderclouds. Under the moon, the sea folding like fishskin. She builds her clothes up, the mirror about to shatter, the ceilings roaring with wind at dawn. Ice turning in its wide bed sky. A long mirror left in a forest, propped up against a beech. At the tip of every twig a distillate. (CM, 87)

In 'Field Theory', Redgrove writes:

> The vast slow weather-whirlpool turns
> And rustles like a young woman's rainy clothes. (AB, 32)

If Redgrove has a fetishized object, it is surely a 'young woman's rainy clothes'. Nothing turns him on more than a drenched white blouse. With Thomas Hardy, it was the rustle of a woman's dress on the heath; for Powys, it was a young sylph's slender limbs, in particular the ankles he ogled on Brighton promenade; for Gide it was a young Arab boy; for Petrarch it was Laura's eyes that drove him mad.

Apart from the womb of a woman, Redgrove eroticizes her clothes more than anything else, especially the eroticism of the partly-open blouse: 'her body open under her throat,/ A laboratory blouse, worn with a white coat/ Chemically clean' he writes in 'The Laboratress' (*Abyssophone*, 30). So many poems are devoted to wet clothes, as in this poem, 'The Clothes Become Magic Wet', where the magician's cloak is magical in itself, a cloak worthy of Prospero or Merlin:

> The magician walks out
> Under the stars in his robes

Smelling of star-jasmine.

This robe generates an aura of charge
Massaged by fold upon fold,
His great hat licks up symbols,

His hem sweeps up the dust,
His clothes are soaked in electrical water
In which, as in the estuary, the stars rise...
(*Sex-Magic-Poetry-Cornwall*, 40)

Redgrove writes poems to the 'wonder-awakening dresses' as he calls them in 'Wardrobe Lady' (SP, 83). They also appear in the short story "Ashiepaddle" (Fear, 140f). The origin of the 'wonder-awakening' nature of the dresses is Penelope Shuttle, Redgrove's Muse. She wore these dresses when Redgrove met her back in the early 70s. There are many poems about Penelope Shuttle's clothes. In "Philosopher and Skin", one of *Eight Alcameos*, he writes of '[p]lenty of wet girls in the mountains, clothed in goddess-skin of mist and waterfall' (EA, 139). In 'The Painter', from *Dressed As For a Tarot Pack*, the wet clothes expand outwards as the woman dreams:

>   she slept sweating wet
> Her bed like piles of clothes that were a river,
> Her sleeping-garment itself alive with water
> Like wet wings folded they stirred, unfolded with a gold
> Unthreading sensation; then swimming her energy at last
> The voice that dwells in the flood calls aloud
> And cries from many waters,
> The streams conversing in the woods
> And the woods talking with their tongues of rain,
> The plasmic garments and the dripping trees
> Branching with sensations as she passes under them
> As if clothed in living mirrors, the clouds above
> Like lantern-slides of the forest. (Tar, 16)

For Redgrove, wet women's clothes signify the height of synæsthetic experience. They seem to be related to the veils and membranes that swaddled the baby in the womb. Clothes-poems include 'A Dewy Garment', 'The Scarf', 'Her Shirt Open', 'Mad Speech Concerning Dress', 'Pneumonia Blouses', 'Dress' and 'Night Light'. In "Second Day" he writes:

> A spurt of juice drenched her garment; now Aphrodite was born from the purple foam. The stained garment flowed down like a shining nakedness. Out of a girl he created the goddess around whose body desire and rapture flowed in the guise of wet clothing. (CM, 44)

In many poems of clothes, the dresses and blouses are the lining of the womb, the woman's sexuality worn over her skin, as if she had been opened inside out. 'It was, as if, in his imagination, he was clothed in his living birth-membranes' (SGH, 47). In 'An Alphaladybet' he writes: '[i]f it is permitted to name the mystery, *she clothes our skins with exterior cunt.*' (Ark, 79) Redgrove relates 'exterior cunt' to Luce Irigaray's notion of women's eroticism being 'all over' the body. In "Rimbaud My Virgil" Redgrove writes of 'the "hysterization of the skin" of the exterior cunt of outer contact seen potentially as deep, intimate and sensuous as the womb experiences of love, masturbation, menstruation, birth' (Rim, 174). The wet clothes may also refer to the placenta, which is one's 'first friend', that thing that one clutches inside the womb, that nourishes one. A soaked shirt held in the hands may create echoes of the placenta. And the cuddly toys of children, or the 'fret blanket' that children have to have to go to sleep, may also be a remnant of the placenta, or the lining of the womb. In 'The Pearl', from *Dressed As For a Tarot Pack*, the foetus is crowned like a princess with the womb's tissues and membranes:

> And when she was born
> She was by the neck of the womb
> As is said 'crowned' and that pearl

> Escaped into the room,
> The room was as though within
> That pearl and walled by it
> When the water rolled
> And broke; she in her drenched
> Uterine garments, the princess
> Crowned...
> (Tar, 45-6)

The womb experience, Redgrove knows as a psychologist, is immensely influential in the individual's life. Making love in wet clothes, swathed in the fluids of eroticism – milk, blood, mucus, saliva, sweat, water, urine, sperm – may be for Redgrove a form of alchemical *regressus ad uterum*. For the post-orgasmic state of dreamtime is like the amniotic suspension in womb-fluids, where the juice from the lover's vulva has magical, prophetic qualities. It is elixir, *soma*, mana, ambrosia, juice from the immortal apple of the Love-Goddess Venus:

> He walks out into his garden, what is this
> Gelatinous alga that wobbles on his lawn after
>
> Contintuous rain? It must be that fat of manna, called
> Maydew, a star-jelly or witch's butter, a ray
>
> Or radiation of a certain star, or its off-scouring
> Cast to earth. But what is it actually? He tastes it,
>
> The oil spreads through the porches of his brain
> Which is now a nest of rainbows. It is exterior soul.
> ('Chemistry', *My Father's Trapdoors*, 35)

A kid, I fell into milk, as the ancient saying goes (Redgrove speaks of 'galactic milk'). In one sense, Redgrove's poems record the journey of falling into this magical, visionary milk of love. The more magical things become in the Redgroverse, the more sensuous, much as Nietzsche spoke of sensuousness increasing with the sense of the tragic. Hypnosis, Redgrove says, needs to be sensuous (SGH, 24).

When wet, Redgrove's clothes are acutely touch-sensitive. So in 'Dress' Redgrove writes:

> Let light bleach the dress; let candle-wax,
> Let all stains drop upon it, let it record
> By dragging streaks the pacing up and down
> In bleaching dyes the droughted summer days,
>
> By plashy blots rut-muddy autumns,
>
> And let this dress register your sweat,
> Your cunt-musk and over its bodice your tears,
>
> Let it play back its recording for a while,
> Let it hover in the bedroom on its hanger;
>
> Softly, you cover my eyes, who have slipped out of it. (Tar, 24)

Clothes are crucial in Redgrove's sensualism, because they cover the skin, which is, as he reminds us, the largest organ of the body. 'Sometimes making love naked could seem like making love in a wonderful house that was unfurnished.' (GF, 21)

If Redgrove had his way, we'd all go 'skyclad', as witches do at their festivals. Then, naked, we'd all feel the air, the wind, the rain, every change in temperature, and the electrostatic/ionization of the clouds. As he says in 'Childstone', 'I can hear better when I am naked' (Tar, 51). We know what he means. So naked moments, such as having a bath, or swimming, are important. Skin on skin is a deep desire of Redgrove's: he writes in 'Mad Speech Concerning Dress':

> My skin
> Needs all skin, his and hers,
> All at once, woven in one stuff, the many faces
> Folding into one Countenance. (AB, 123)

Peter Redgrove: Here Comes the Flood

Again and again in Redgrove's work, we see the desire for unity, for wholeness. He is always talking of the *whole* house, the *whole* body, the *whole* world. This desire stems from a belief in the unity of things, which is perhaps the primary idea of magic.

In *The Black Goddess*, Redgrove creates a poetry of clothes. He speaks of clothes as able to control the weather systems of the body – the blouse opening at the neck controls the air and scent and so on flowing around the body (BG, 66f). He focuses continually on the V-neck opening of a shirt or blouse, likening it to the vulva. By opening her shirt, a woman can make the world magical. This is the latent meaning of the poem 'Her Shirt Open', where even a 'slate-lined alley' becomes '[e]rotic and holy' (IHS, 10):

> She opens her shirt, which is wet
> And heavy with its drink like a superb silk,
> And a eerie feeling superimposes
> From the stone electricity and that vertical smile,
> Like another music, or echoes
> Exploring buildings not yet visible,
> The metallic echoes of the slate-lined alley
> Erotic and holy, as when we watched
> The slow-growing sea-drowned grass
> And she turned to me again, her shirt open,
> And the current changed around us, and in the canal
> The underwater forests switched direction
> Showing that sluices far away had opened up
> New reaches of the waterway, with varying tides. (IHS, 9-10)

Another erotic evocation of clothes occurs in 'Electrical Sisters', where Redgrove melds the feel of air and wind with clothes and beds, so that the feeling of one's clothes and one's bed is a spirit familiar, a being who wraps themselves around you. Your clothes, your bed, the air surrounding your body become an 'electrical sister', a creature who never leaves you, a special form of the witch's familiar, your body aura:

> The wind entering your clothes
> Like somebody getting into bed with you
> Sliding on your sheety sleeves
>
> Wrapping your skirt around your legs,
> Somebody electrical, who loves light blue,
> With this aura of mild blue electricity;
>
> The pleasure of sharing the clothes
> With this spirited wind that crackles them
> Shines from your eyes in sky blue. (Sex, 42)

Redgrove's poetry of clothes makes garments extraordinary – but not in the flashy, materialistic, sexy-superficial way of the catwalk, of *Vogue* and multinational corporations. Sadly, these consumer-driven forms of clothing pander to masculinist notions of what is 'sexy' and marketing at its most pornographic, unable to disguise its avaricious ethic which is founded on the dollar. No amount of gloss can hide the dross of 'high fashion'. It's as if fashion and style were, in the Redgrovean system, debased alchemical matter, mere unrefined putrefaction: faeces rather than gold, capitalist-consumerist anal greed gone to dust.

Peter Redgrove: Here Comes the Flood

Magic

Imagination is the most scientific of the faculties, because it alone understands universal analogy, or what a mystic religion calls correspondence.

Charles Baudelaire[12]

There is something huge, vast and infinite in Redgrove's poetry, usually symbolized by the stars, sea and clouds. He uses the basic tenet of magic – *as above, so below* – which comes from the Emerald Table of Hermes Trismegistus.[9] Basically, the hermetic tenet says that everything on Earth reflects everything in Heaven. Or, more accurately and psychologically, inner and outer are connected, even identical. In feminism, the personal is political. So the intimate, private orgasmic union of two lovers is identical with the public, worldly energies of weather and Nature. This is fundamental to Western magic, this sense of unity in all things, so the stars can influence human lives (in astrology), or certain colours can influence certain acts, or certain herbs can help certain emotions to be produced, etc. The basic theory of magical correspondences, employed by Baudelaire in his poem 'Correspondances' occurs through Western art – in Shakespeare, in alchemy, Neoplatonism, and in Oriental mysticisms such as Taoism, where the Tao is the Way and the One, something akin to 'the One' of Neoplatonism.

> La Nature est un temple où de vivants piliers
> Laissent parfois sortir de confuses paroles;
> L'homme y passe à travers des forêts de symboles
> Qui l'observent avec des regards familiers.
>
> Comme de longs échos qui de loin se confondent
> Dans une ténébreuse et profonde unité,
> <u>Vaste comme la nuit</u> et comme la clarté,

---
12 Baudelaire, letter to Toussenel, quoted in John Pilling: *Modern European Poets*, Pan 1982, 16

Les parfums, les couleurs et les sons se répondent.

Il est des parfums frais comme des chairs d'enfants,
Doux comme les hautbois, verts comme les prairies,
— Et d'autres, corrompus, riches et triomphants,

Ayant l'expansion des choses infinies,
Comme l'ambre, le musc, le benjoin et l'encens,
Qui chantent les transports de l'esprit et des sens.[13]

Novalis writes illuminatingly of poetic connections in a way which applies not only to Redgrove but to most poets:

> In our mind, everything is connected in the most peculiar, pleasant, and lively manner. The strangest things come together by virtue of one space, one time, an odd similarity, an error, some accident. In this manner, curious unities and peculiar connections originate - one thing reminds us of everything, becomes the sign of many things. Reason and imagination are united through time and space in the most extraordinary manner, and we can say that each thought, each phenomenon of our mind is the most individual part of an altogether individual totality. (*Novalis Schriften.* 3, 650-1)

Redgrove's is a poetry of correspondences, as is all poetry, a spider's web of correspondences, crisscrossing the world laterally, like the net or cluster of jewels in Buddhism. So a woman's body can be her house (in *The Alchemical Journal*), or the touch of a lover can be like the caress of the stars. Inner and outer commingle. Redgrove's poetic correspondence is part of that alternative to Western established religion: alchemy, tassomancy, astrology,

---

[13] 'Nature is a temple where living pillars Let sometimes emerge confused words; Man crosses it through forests of symbols Which watch him with intimate eyes. Like those deep echoes that meet from afar In a dark and profound harmony, As vast as night and clarity, So perfumes, colors, tones answer each other. There are perfumes fresh as children's flesh, Soft as oboes, green as meadows, And others, corrupted, rich, triumphant, Possessing the diffusion of infinite things, Like amber, musk, incense and aromatic resin, Chanting the ecstasies of spirit and senses.' (tr. G. Wagner, *Selected Poems of Charles Baudelaire*, Grove Press, 1974).

cheiromancy, geomancy, Gnosticism, witchcraft, angelism, Rosicrucianism, Neoplatonism – all those cults, movements and beliefs which form the 'underbelly' of Western religion, which seem to be in opposition to Christianity, but which in fact fuse with Christianity at many points. (In the story "The Three Feathers" Redgrove spoofs these obscure beliefs, speaking of 'decimatomancy': '[d]ivination by killing one in ten', and 'massacromancy': '[d]ivination by killing everybody'[14] These beliefs are 'occult' but normal – that is, they occur everyplace but are suppressed or hidden away. In his fiction Redgrove explores these fringe or occult areas. In *The God of Glass* he works through realms of heresy and ritual made (in)famous by the 1973 film *The Exorcist*. In *The Beekeepers*, the protagonists try all manner of 'paranormal' activities, from dowsing to planchette to sex magic. In *In the Country of the Skin*, Sandy speaks of '[v]isions created them by the one energy of many names: love, sex, dreaming, perversion, art, womb, geology, god, justice, cruelty, atomic hydrogen, galactic milk, celestial holography, poetry, magick.' (ICS, 10-11) The search is for the 'Something More Than This' which people sense is there. Something vast and powerful in life, but which is invisible, and suppressed:

> We still want there to be something. I think we don't really care whether it is an illusion or not, so long as it is a grand illusion. We go from guru to guru, from sham to shaman, from confidence man to hypnotist to magician to new wave priest to megalithic stone circles to tantric yoga to Tai-Chi to alchemy to Jungian psychology – and all the way back again via dowsing and animal magnetism. (101)

Redgrove has explored many of these 'occult' pathways, and speaks enthusiastically of yoga, hypnotism, homeopathy, dowsing and sexual magic. In amongst the talk of 'Bee-cults' in the novel *The Facilitators* a character says 'I find the bee-hum hypnotic. Humming perks you up like nothing else I know.' (63)

---
14 *The One Who Set to Study Fear*, 90

Peter Redgrove: Here Comes the Flood

Starting with weather – an agreeably neutral topic (though not really neutral at all) – Redgrove shows in *The Black Goddess and the Sixth Sense* that so many 'occult' experiences are in fact normal. Redgrove takes the magic founded by Dionysius the Areopagite, Dante, Agrippa, Paracelsus, John Dee, the Qabbalah, Sufic mysticism, Gnosticism, Plato, Aristotle, Pythagoras, Hermes Trismegistus, etc, and makes it homely. That is, he brings it into the home, instead of leaving it in the secret laboratory, or the windswept hilltop, or the coven in the glade of some obscure forest.

In the 'theory of correspondences' (Baudelaire's 'forest of symbols'), everything connects together. So we can move, intuitively (poetically) from angels to planets to plants to numbers to jewels to minerals to humours to days to colours to elements to planets and round and round again. Sections of Redgrove's *The Alchemical Journal* are pure magic, they read like treatises on occultism, as in no.15:

> Bricks in Staines, the small Roman bricks, numerous as the leaves on the trees, a world of smells and angels, angels behind their wings of smell, the smell of an angel wafted to me by the soft movement of its wings, says the Book of Lambsprink, and my hammers are the seven planets with which I forge beautiful things. The fire of our stars lies hidden in our substances.

There is more alchemy, magic, hermeticism and conscious symbol-making in Redgrove than in most modern poets. One thinks of Yeats and Graves, who both created magical systems. One could happily read Robert Graves' work without needing notes, but it helps enormously in the depth of understanding of his poems if one can also dip into *The White Goddess*. It's a question of levels, how deep one wishes to go. It's the same with Redgrove. Although he terms all his poetry as strange-but-ordinary, it does help if one knows something of magic, occultism and psychology.

This century it is C.G. Jung who has done more to bring together magic, mysticism, religion, psychology and science than any other individual (one thinks also of J.G. Frazer, Mircea Eliade, Freud, Erich Neumann). In Jung's marvellous *Collected Works* one can leap from subjects such as Gnosticism to Chinese alchemy, or from *animus* possession to the *Book of Job*. Redgrove follows in this wide-ranging Jungian tradition. Redgrove's philosophy is firmly in the Jung-Eliade-Layard tradition.

There are three worlds or states of being in Redgrove's mythopoeia:

World	Imagery
Upper, higher, transcendent realm	stars, clouds, ocean, wind
Middle, day-to-day realm	people, societies, events
Lower, underworld, 'underlife'	'dark senses', sex, orgasm

The poet is the shaman who unites these three realms. The archaic shaman climbs the World Tree, the Cosmic Tree or *axis mundi* which links the three ontological realms. The poet travels between the worlds. Look at Rilke, Rimbaud, Shakespeare or Dante – you'll see them making these spiritual journeys all the time. What Redgrove is trying to do is to join the three realms together, so that the higher or transcendent realm is not off-limits like the Christian Heaven, something to be had after death, but to bring it into the everyday world, to pull Heaven down from the clouds and bring it into the home, into our everyday lives. Similarly, that dark under-realm, presided over by the Black Goddess, is also brought into the everyday space. Poetry (and love) melts these realms together. So everything is pulled in, by the electromagnetism of poetry, into the womb-space, into the Celtic cauldron of the Sow-Goddess of Wales, Cerwidden, into the alchemical vessel which is the womb of the beloved woman.

Peter Redgrove: Here Comes the Flood

Redgrove, like Luce Irigaray, reveres the womb-experience. Irigaray writes of the special relationship women have with the 'spatial' and the 'foetal'.[15]

So poetry is essential in the manufacture of a life. It is essential to make art because art can join together all experiences, all zones, all ontologies. Or, if you don't make art, then meditate, or make love, or do something creative. One must write, though, always, as the French feminist Hélène Cixous says in her essay "The Laugh of the Medusa", which is probably the most important feminist text for Redgrove, and for many feminists, because it is so energizing and inspiring.

So, in the poetics, the unification, which is the very basis of magic, is symbolized in Redgrove by the constant references to the stars and clouds and oceans of the upper world, and to the black, unknown, secret, intimate sensations, which are the inner/ underworld things. Few poets have written so gloriously, for example, of stars. I can think of Rilke, who throws out gorgeous, rich starscapes, especially in the *Duino Elegies*, and Shakespeare, where in every play there is always that sense of the vast heavens wheeling overhead. Here is Redgrove's 'The Wheel':

>...and the universe
> In me turns, the sails of stars
> Flapping and dripping radiance,
>
> The pricked sheets of constellations
> Through which we see total light... (Man, 92-3)

Rilke's stars are not mere 'backdrops' to stylish poesie, but

---

15 Irigaray in "Sexual difference", lecture, 1982, writes: 'Freud's statement that her stage is oral is significant but still exiles her from her most archaic and constituent site. No doubt the word 'oral' is particularly useful in describing a woman: morphologically she has two mouths and two pairs of lips. But she can only act on this morphology and create something from it if she retains her relationship to the *spatial* and the *foetal*.' *The Irigaray Reader*, 170

are juicy, tangy, edible things. Redgrove, too, creates juicy stars: isn't that amazing – *wet* stars, stars drenched in water? (See the extract from 'Living in Falmouth', Part IX, quoted above). Redgrove washes his hair in starlight in 'To the Water-Psychiatrist' (Man, 25). The wardrobe-lady too is full of stars – '[s]he has combed star-rays into a shaggy night-dress' (SP, 83). Of course, stars are a natural manifestation of the Goddess, for the Goddess is Mother Night, called Nut in Egyptian mythology. In the famous illustration from thousands of years ago, the Goddess Nut stretches above the Earth in a curve.

In Rilke and Redgrove, stars are not only 'out there', in the black sky, they are also 'in here', in the black inner sky. The two places are the same. Air too is a symbol or manifestation for Redgrove of powerful outer/ innerness. Air is what gives the body its 'skin orgasm', so you can't ignore air, and in many poems Redgrove writes of air, or the wind, which is another form of the great 'invisible' which is all around us, ignored but always there. In 'Streets of the Spirits' he writes: 'I think of the air like an immense cope/ Of silky glass stirred by the valiant trees' (*The Apple-Broadcast*, 39). Ted Hughes writes, correctly, that '[a]lmost every good poet, when he mentions the wind, touches one of his good moments of poetry.' (*Poetry in the Making*, 33) Redgrove speaks of pylons 'choiring in the wind', a phenomena anyone can appreciate if they've stood in a cornfield over which the pylons march, buzzing like bees ('Transactions', Man, 50). Redgrove gleefully connects the electromagnetic energy of the pylons with a cosmic vision of the Earth, moon and sun:

> The pylons choiring in the wind
> Marching like the X-rays of cathedrals
> Along their zesty ozone spoor like the odour of mushrooms,
> The earth spinning within its mother, the waters,
> Around its father, the sun,
> Within clear sight of its godmother,
> The mob-capped, nectar-rayed moon.

In the poem 'Air', Redgrove writes of '[t]he air from the inside darkness', moving from the sensual experience of air and wind to the poetic and mythical associations of all things aerodynamic (Man, 110-111):

> Blowing breath at each other,
> The air from the inside darkness
> Palpitates with the heartbeats,
> And it is living air. It is
> An invisible quicksilver flowing
> Round your fingers as you touch.
> Its touch is very great,
>
> It is a diffused flesh, breathed from the warmth
> And the darkness inside which is not dark at all,
> Any more than the night of stars is dark,
> Black, without darkness.

If water is Redgrove's first element, air is his second, because air carries his primary sense, scent. Like the sea, the air too is infinite and eternally mobile. So in *A Crystal of Industrial Time*, Redgrove writes of 'a perfumer's shop-cloud [which] surrounds me with its samples breaking over my shoulders' (CIT, 61). The imagery here recalls many of those in Patrick Süskind's novel *Perfume*.[16] Otherness, the other world, is dark and may connect us with senses other than the visual: with smell, for instance:

> The other world comes through with a certain note
> Which may be a perfume.
> ('Superstition', WNP, 98)

It is the synæsthesia of Baudelaire, where the poet becomes one with the object of contemplation. Baudelaire writes in *Artificial Paradises*:

---

[16] Patrick Süskind: *Perfume*, Penguin 1987

> Your eye fastens upon a tree... something that would be a most natural comparison in the poet's mind, will become a reality in yours. First, you will attribute your passions, longings, and sadness to the tree; its moaning and swaying will become your own; and by and by, you are the tree itself. (55)

Baudelaire's synæsthesia is nothing new in poetry – Sappho was writing of love as a wind shaking oaks on a mountainside two thousand years ago. But Baudelaire's new, orgasmic sense of metaphor rejuvenated poetry dramatically:

> There are perfumes as fresh as children's flesh,
> As soft as oboes, as green as meadows
> – And others, corrupt, costly, and masterful,
> Having the power of infinite things,
> Like amber, musk, Benjamin, and frankincense,
> Which sing out the rapture of spirit and senses.
> ('Correspondences', *Oeuvres completes*, I, 113)

In Baudelaire's poetry of *jouissance* there is 'a paroxysm of identification' (Kristeva, *Tales*, 333), an identification between 'cause and effect, subject and object, mesmerist and one entranced', writes Baudelaire in *Paradis artificiel* (27). In Baudelairean synæsthesia, the poetic metaphor is wielded as a tool, a way of achieving synæsthesia. John Lechte, discussing Julia Kristeva, the feminist with whom Redgrove has most in common perhaps, writes:

> In Baudelaire, it is the theme of perfume which would most closely proximate the notion of metaphor as condensation – as love. According to Kristeva, perfume has fusional connotations that condense the intoxicated memory of an invaded maternal body.' Perfume gives the Baudelairean text its great lyricism by dissolving the object, or rather by merging all objects into one: the poet's contemplation, the poet's subjectivity as a subject in process. Baudelaire's contemplation thus becomes the equivalent of condensation – of metaphor – as such. ("Art, Love, and Melancholy", in Lechte, ed, 30-31)

Peter Redgrove: Here Comes the Flood

Easy to see how this notion of Baudelairean condensation and metaphor applies to Redgrove, who is very much a poet in the Baudelairean-synæsthetic tradition. (Baudelaire had his own 'Black Goddess', his lover Jeanne Duval, the 'black Venus', whom he eulogized as Muse, Madonna and Guardian Angel). Julia Kristeva writes in "Baudelaire, or Infinity, Perfume, and Punk":

> Perfume is thus the most powerful metaphor for that archaic universe, preceding sight, where what takes place is the conveyance of the most opaque lovers' indefinite identities, together with the chilliest words: 'There are strong perfumes for all matter/ Is porous. They seem to penetrate glass.' (*Tales of Love*, 334)

Like Ted Hughes, Redgrove is an immensely *elemental* poet, which is also how one might describe Shakespeare, Shelley, Vaughan and Sappho, for the elements are always raging through these poets. In Redgrove, all these strands of experience are unified. So we cannot speak of water, for example, without also bringing in eroticism, women, storms, electricity, ecstasy, skin, alchemy, science, wombs, birth, etc. One of my favourite experiences in Redgrove's work of air and scent – and water and touch – is the opening of the poem 'Harvest', (FE, 14), which fuses eroticism, touch, colour, symbolism, alchemy, perfume, the feminine, nature and synæsthesia:

> The greatest possible touch, to bathe.
> The wind bathing in the wheat,
> The great invisible woman plunges
> Into the heavy tassels, into the wheat-smell
> That is like straw baskets full of new bread;
> The wheat splashes round her, it must cry out,
> All the stems chafing, like an immense piano plunged into
> Which continues playing as she swims...

You've all the senses here, powerfully – and systematically, in the Rimbaudian sense – evoked (BG, 122f). Bathing in wheat – there's a glorious experience! And very erotic too, but erotic in the expansive, cosmic sense, not in the sense of life-limiting pornography. And alchemical too – the image recalls alchemical gold, and the red of blood/ passion/ energy/ life itself. And also, this image of wheat recalls the final ecstasy and unifying vision of Wolf in John Cowper Powys' novel *Wolf Solent,* where the protagonist plunges his hands into the Byzantine gold, Cimmerian gold and Saturnian gold of a wheatfield.[17] Yet all this golden splendour comes from the black Earth, and this is what Redgrove tries to nourish: the sense of rebirth from darkness, from what he calls 'the dark senses' or underworld. The line in 'Considering the Whites' shows that Redgrove, like D.H. Lawrence in 'Bavarian Gentians', believes that darkness is the rich source of life:

> Our flowers are echoes of deep strata, twinklings from black afar.
> (WNP, 83)

Underworld, Underlife

> *There is the inner life, which is the world of final reality, the world of memory, emotion, imagination, intelligence, and natural common sense, and which goes on all the time, consciously or unconsciously, like the heart beat. There is also the thinking process by which we break into that inner life and capture answers and evidence to support the answers out of it. That process or raid, or persuasion, or ambush, or dogged hunting, or surrender, is the kind of thinking we have to learn and if we do not somehow learn it, then our minds lie in us like the fish in the pond of a man who cannot fish.*
>
> Ted Hughes, *Poetry in the Making* (57-58)

---

17 Powys: *Wolf Solent,* op.cit., 632

Peter Redgrove: Here Comes the Flood

Peter Redgrove makes a mythopoeia out of the 'dark senses' (BG, 94), which he terms *horasis,* carnal knowledge, *le rêve,* the sixth sense, William Blake's Fifth Window, or *Daath.* In *The Sleep of the Great Hypnotist* it is called 'creating a Sphinx':

> I will have the eyes of a hawk or a lynx, the nose of a dog or a jackal, the hearing of a gazelle, the touch of a dolphin, that extends through the ocean. (71)

The creative visions, as Sandy says (*In the Country of the Skin,* 10-11), come from 'one energy with many names: love, sex, dreaming, perversion, art, womb, geology, god, justice, cruelty, atomic hydrogen, galactic milk, celestial holography, poetry, magick.'

The drive of *The Black Goddess* is this: that life is enriched when you actively engage extra-sensuous perception. Redgrove draws on a tradition, that goes back a long way: to the Irish and Welsh bards described by Robert Graves in *The White Goddess,* to the great Arabic and Sufi poets (Rumi, Jami, Rabi'a, al-Hallaj, Attar), and, more recently, to the Romantics, the extra-sensuously perceptive poets: Goethe, Novalis, Coleridge, Wordsworth, and post-Symbolists such as Rimbaud, Rilke, Yeats and St-John Perse.

Like Aldous Huxley, who drew together many different strands of mysticism for his book *The Perennial Philosophy,* or J.G. Frazer making a compendium of myths in his *The Golden Bough,* Redgrove brings together many different types of extra-sensuous perception – from yoga, meditation, High Magic, day-dreaming and sleep. Jung too had this kind of comprehensive or encyclopaedical approach. It annoys purists, though, who claim you can't lump the absolutist monism of Sufism with the annihilation of Buddhist *nirvana,* for example. For critics and purists, ecstasies don't mix, they are contextually-bound, and stem from and go towards different sources and goals.[18]

For religionists, theologians and mystics, it is abhorrent to confuse the Islamic dissolution of self in Allah ('Extinction of Extinction' says al-Ghazzali)[19] with the Catholic self-God union ('He has allowed me to taste his sweetness' gasps St Teresa of Avila).[20] In Sufic mystical ecstasy, there is no 'union', as if self and Allah were getting into bed with each other, existing on the same plane. The soul is not on an equal standing with Allah in Islam. There is simply oblivion, and the mystic is drawn to Allah like the moth expiring in a candle flame, to use a famous analogy.[21] For Christians and Westerners, there is always something of the self, the ego, retained in the *unio mystica*. Well, what Redgrove does is to take the psychological approach of Jung and naturalize it. That is, to study not the goals of ecstasy, or the socio-religious contexts, but the psycho-physical effects on the individual, on emotions and the body. That way, one can compare the ecstasies of Hindu *samadhi*, Zen *satori*, Sufic bliss, Buddhist *nirvana* or Buddhahood, daydreams, hypnagogia, trances, Meister Eckhart's 'God-intoxication', St Teresa's rapture, etc. Psychology broadens the fields of enquiry, and links together religion, magic, mythology, art, visions, poetry, theology, occultism, etc. One is free to move about in all directions, because one focuses on the individual. Redgrove's mythopoeia is founded on the individual, and is not part of establishment religion (although you might say that magic/ occultism/ hermeticism is a kind of establishment – now going through a new manifestation with the 'New Age' phenomenon).

Redgrove's connections with mysticism are obvious: when *The*

---

[18] see R.C. Zaehner: *Mysticism Sacred and Profane*, Oxford University Press, 1957
[19] Al-Ghazzali, quoted in F.C. Happold,260
[20] St Teresa, *The Interior Castle*, tr J.M. Cohen, Penguin, quoted in Happold, 346
[21] see A.J. Arberry: *Sufism*, Allen & Unwin 1979

Cloud of Unknowing talks about the 'dart of longing love' amidst divine darkness, that is Redgrove's unconscious senses; when the wonderful Jan van Ruysbroeck writes in *The Adornment of Spiritual Marriage* that '[a]ll the riches which are in God by nature we possess by way of love in God, and God in us', that is the realization of the 'magic' of life which Redgrove talks about, the reawakening of the divine in Nature, in us. Meister Eckhart too speaks of the identification with God and the sacred, as Rimbaud did, and if we quote from a few of Eckhart's sermons and tractates, we can see how close Redgrove is to mediæval mysticism:

> I am the cause that God is God... I say, God must be very I, I very God, so consummately one that this he and this I are one *is*, in this is-ness working one work eternally... To talk about the world as being made by God tomorrow, yesterday, would be talking nonsense. God makes the world and all things in this present now.[22]

Redgrove's 'unknowing' or 'synæsthetic plenum of the unconscious or subliminal senses' (BG, 123) is found in all religions and mysticisms. To cater for all eventualities, Redgrove gives his pellucid apperception different names, linking it with Tantrism, Gnosticism (the Goddess Sophia), ritual magicke, yoga, alchemy, etc.

Ted Hughes writes in *Poetry in the Making*:

> ...this is a gift we all share, potentially, that it is simply one of the characteristics of being alive in these mysterious electrical bodies of ours, and the difficult thing is not to pick up the information but to recognise it – to accept it into our consciousness. (123)

He calls this extra-sensuous perception the Black Goddess, of which more later. It is the 'underlife' of Powys, the underworld where Isis, Jesus and Orpheus go. They travel to recover life itself, to be reborn. Orpheus goes for his spirit familiar, his *anima*, his

---
22 Eckhart, *Sermon* XCIX, *Tractate* II, *Sermon* LXXXIII, in Happold, 273-9

inspiration, his Muse, his Goddess, his alchemical counterpart, Eurydice (a journey most eloquently lyricized in Rilke's great poem 'Orpheus. Eurydice. Hermes').

In Redgrove the fundamental journey is death and rebirth, symbolized every month by the menstrual cycle. Robert Graves related the death and rebirth of the poet to the ancient god or consort of the Goddess, who was ritually sacrificed on the Midsummer pyres and reborn as the Christ child at the Winter Solstice or Christmas. This is what Graves calls the Prime Theme or monomyth.[23] Redgrove concurs with this death-rebirth journey, writing: 'goddess-worship means: transformation and rebirth' (BG, xxiv). And Redgrove's contemporary, Ted Hughes, has analyzed all of Shakespeare's work on the basis of Graves' monomyth.

The egg in menstruation dies and is reborn, like the poet, like the consort of the Goddess, like the woman herself, who is fragmented then reconstituted every Moon. The menstrual dimension is as important for Redgrove as alchemy or weather-sensitivity. The poem 'Silver Woman' mixes biology and poetry vividly:

> The moon-dew melts, the orgasm
> At the period, that red crystal
> High in the belly that rolls its droplets
> Down, and as the dark flesh becomes blood,
> Shews; a little bloody-bell sounds in the belly. (Tar, 41)

The nature of blackness in Redgrove is not that of Shakespeare's Dark Lady, who was 'as black as hell' (sonnet 147.14). Shakespeare's one-time Muse was a Black Goddess, but of the ferocious, devouring kind, where women are seen from the misogynist, patriarchal perspective as the 'gateway to hell', as Tertullian and other Christian fathers say. Shakespeare's Dark

---

23 Graves: *The White Goddess*, op.cit., 341, 488; *Poetic Craft*, op.cit., 109; *Steps*, op.cit., 113

Lady is partly fierce because she is the projection of the poet's anxieties concerning that highly-charged erotic entanglement between the poet, the Fair Youth and the woman.[24]

In patriarchal religion, these concepts conjoin: death-women-vagina-hell-decay-sin-sex. Redgrove's 'underworld' is similarly a female space, though purged of patriarchal hatred, for Redgrove has embraced the so-called 'dark side' of people and sexuality. Redgrove's is a thoroughly heterosexual vision of life, however, and he is, like Robert Graves, sometimes sexist, because he thinks in dualities, in terms of masculine-feminine and men-women. As French feminists such as Hélène Cixous have shown, these dualist terms are reductive, they limit life. But Redgrove also says, '[o]ne must think in terms of a continuum, not binary logic.'[25]

In Redgrove, black is associated with many of the usual things in occult philosophy: night, Mother Night, Black Goddess, *yin*, Kali-Yuga (night in Indian mythology), the superdazzling darkness of Catholicism (in St John of the Cross, *The Cloud of Unknowing*, etc), witchcraft, prophecy, blood mysteries, alchemy, etc. Black is the state before regeneration, the space before time, the place of seeds and wombs. Blackness is supremely the Goddess's space, the 'moon-place' as Redgrove calls it, where creations occur. Novalis, in *Hymnen an die Nacht*, wrote of the feminine Night, the vastness that encircles life, which is the Black Goddess:

> Heavenly as flashing stars
> In each vastness
> Appear the infinite eyes
> Which the Night open in us. (*Pollen*, 138-140)

---

[24] see Hyder Rollins, ed: *A New Variorum Edition of Shakespeare: The Sonnets*, 2 vols, Lippincott, Philadelphia, 1944; Joseph Pequingey: *Such Is My Love: A Study of Shakespeare's Sonnets,* University of Chicago Press, Chicago 1985

[25] letter, 19 May 1993

Peter Redgrove: Here Comes the Flood

D.H. Lawrence often wrote of seeds buried in the soil, waiting to grow – in *The Rainbow* Lawrence describes Will Brangwen's state thus:

> Suddenly, like a chestnut falling out of a burr, he was shed naked and glistening on to soft, fecund earth, leaving behind him the hard rind of worldly knowledge and experience.[26]

Redgrove doesn't rate Lawrence highly as an influence, but this motif of the seed under the ground in soft, dark soil waiting to grow is archetypal Redgrove, really. Seeds appear in 'Lunar Mane', where all those storms and rainfalls beloved of Redgrove are associated clearly with the Goddess. In this poem, the Goddess appears as the controller of the weather, as the Goddess was in ancient times the creator of such powers:

> Low thunder and flashes of lightning
> Emitted by her in lunar cycle; the rich clouds
> Pass over the full moon... (IHS, 35)

The Goddess here is like the Chinese dragon, which brings storms and rain when it flies by. The dragon is a powerful embodiment of feminine mysteries, and one sees dragonish alchemy seething throughout Redgrove's poetry – in "Dragon and Mistress", for example, where Falmouth Library and Museum becomes a dragon (CM, 83), and the child sees the dragonish shapes in the womb. What is clear by now is that there are more important things for Redgrove than magic, poetry, yoga, alchemy, landscape or weather-sensitivity, and that is the Goddess, or love, or women.

In the terms of French feminism, Redgrove's 'mother-world' is the pre-verbal, pre-oedipal space of the mother: Redgrove is trying, to use the terminology of French feminism, to rewrite the maternal body. Redgrove's 'mother-world' is like Julia Kristeva's

---
26 Lawrence: *The Rainbow*, Penguin 1986, 185

notion of the dark, pre-oedipal space of the mother, which she calls the *chora*. Michael Payne defines Kristeva's *chora* thus: 'a nourishing and maternal, pre-verbal semiotic space or state in which the linguistic sign has not yet been articulated as the absence of an object' (239). Redgrove's 'mother-world' is, like Kristeva's *chora*, founded on the maternal body as an actuality. As Kristeva writes in *Desire in Language*: '[c]ells fuse, split, and proliferate; volumes grow, tissues stretch, and body fluids change rhythm, speeding up or slowing down. Within the body, growing as a graft, indomitable, there is an other' (237). The 'other' is the child; the poet in Redgrove's is pregnant with a different sort of child: her/ his art, the poem, the artwork as the Magical Child of alchemy.

In *Revolution as Poetic Language*, Kristeva speaks of the *chora* as the place where 'the subject is both generated and negated' (28); it is 'a place of change, it is fluid, amorphous, 'pre-word', and, like a cell, divisible' (ib., 239-240n.). Language, though, can never circumscribe this maternal space: to name it is to change it. So Redgrove is always pointing or suggesting, for poets know how fragile these things are, how easily destroyed by the wrong words, the wrong act, the wrong thoughts.

Four

Feminism and the Goddess

I am Nature, the Mother of all
Mistress of the elements,
Sovereign of the Spirit,
Queen of the Dead,
Queen of the Immortals,
The single embodiment of all goddesses and gods
...I am Isis.

Isis, in Apuleius' *Metamorphoses* (in Nicholson, 91)

[the Black Goddess is] *the world's hope-in-love...the symbol and gateway to everything we could know in the apparent blackness beyond visible sight... [she is] 'the goddess of clairvoyance, clear-seeing and second sight...the lover's light of touch in bed, and the dark night of touch in the womb. She is the Goddess of Intimacy, of being 'in touch' and of that fifth window, the skin...*

Peter Redgrove, *The Black Goddess*, 136-7

She's Here

The Goddess is reappearing for poets, neo-pagans, New Agers, hippies, artists, writers, witches and magicians. 'There is no question in my mind that the Goddess is reawakening,' says Merlin Stone.[27] The Goddess is the alternative to the Judaeo-Christian God, to the jealous Biblical Father-God, the tyrant of patriarchy, the old man with the white beard who presides over the male mysteries of brotherhood and violence. The Goddess is the embodiment of feminine mysteries and female energy. She is politically green, ecologically gentle, the Mother Earth, the Mother of us all, a reaction against greedy multinational conglomerates, against egotistical white Anglo-Saxon first world Americanized corporate capitalist materialist consumerist Imperialist urban-centred money-driven culture.

The Goddess became really popular with the rise of feminism and counter-culture in the 1960s. She was there before that – in Robert Graves, Bachofen, Neumann, Jung, Frazer, Briffault and others. One can see the Goddess in Shakespeare, Hardy, Lawrence, Rilke, Sappho, Novalis, Spenser, Drayton, Petrarch, Dante, the troubadours, all manner of mediæval poets, in the poets of ancient Egypt, Babylon, Sumer, India, China, etc. Historically, the Goddess is the powerful deity of the ancient and Classical era, with names like Isis, Ishtar, Demeter, Venus, Sophia, Venus, Kali, etc. Before the historic era, there was the rise of agriculture and that sacred identification of women-Earth-fertility-seasons, etc, embodied in those headless and nameless figurines of prehistoric times, the so-called stone "Venuses". Before the prehistoric era, no one knows just how far back Goddess worship goes, although, significantly, there is no father-figure in prehistory: '[t]here is no trace of a father figure in any of the Paleolithic periods. The life-creating power seems to have

---

27 Merlin Stone, in Shirley Nicholson, ed

been of the Great Goddess alone', writes Marija Gimbutas (316). No father figure! This is a blow to followers of Freud, Lacan, Hamlet and Oedipus!

Geoffrey Ashe has written of the elements of the Goddess in the Virgin Mary: he describes how he interpreted Graves' *The White Goddess* thus:

> *The White Goddess*...was ahead of its time. As is well known, Graves's usual publishers turned it down. But the book came into its own in the Goddess revival, which it helped to inspire. Like many readers, I had great difficulty with it. Eventually I more or less grasped what Graves was driving at, including the idea – later developed by him and others, and now widely current –that all the Goddess-figures of myth and cult are aspects or manifestations of 'the Goddess', the ultimate female Power or Energy, hinted at in Goethe's *Ewig-Weibliche* at the end of *Faust*: once accorded supreme honour under countless names and in countless forms, but pushed into the background by male deities, demoted and split up...to humanity's loss. The Goddess is not thought of as simply God with a gender change, she is different in kind. She is within Nature, not 'external to it'; she is the Earth-Mother, with priority over the Sky-Father, who is an usurper; she is the universal life-giver, mistress of animals, Muse of inspiration, creator and destroyer; to be encountered, not argued about metaphysically. Pascal wrote that the God of his mystical experience was not the God of the philosophers. (*Discovering the Goddess*)

For Goddess poets such as Redgrove and Robert Graves, the Goddess was usurped by men in the Classical age, and male deities were set up in her stead: Apollo, Dionysus, Jesus, Jehovah. For Redgrove and Chris Knight, men took over women's mysteries – the blood mysteries of menstruation, sexuality and childbirth.[28] For Redgrove and Knight, men (or more accurately, masculine society) stole women's power, creating a patriarchal state of law, and the basis of the struggle was in powergaming centred on sex.[2] By the methods we have come to know and love

---

[28] Chris Knight: *Blood Relations*, Yale University Press, New Haven, 1991

– violence, force, coercion, persuasion, propaganda and dogma – men took social and emotional power away from women. The patriarchal quality of Western culture since that time has been determined by this white noise of disinformation concerning sexuality, menstruation, pregnancy, conception, child rearing, the family and work.

The resurgence of the Goddess, then, is the religious dimension, you might say, of feminism. The Goddess is a new spiritual development centred on an ancient spiritual feeling, a way of living that is dynamic and empowering, healing and nurturing. There are many books on the Goddess around now – by Gadon, Sjöo, Woodman, Matthews, Walker, Harding, Warner, etc. And many artists who use the Goddess in their images and sculptures: Judy Chicago, Sant-Phalle, Schapiro, Bourgeois, Edelson, Sherwood, Craighead, Marisol and McCoy. Judy Chicago says her aim is 'to make the feminine holy'.[29] Goddess philosophy is about holism, healing, energizing, visioning, empathy, earthing, weaving, nurturance, compassion, union, emotion – there is a new language being created to cater for the anti-patriarchal nature of the Goddess cult.[30]

The Goddess movement is a small but powerful part of Western culture – linked with postwar movements such as the rise of witchcraft (again), UFOlogy, Tarot, Buddhism, astrology, earth magic, ley lines, all kinds of 'occultism', while on the other side, Goddess worship is centred in radical feminism, in the marvellous work of feminists such as Mary Daly and Barbara G. Walker.

What has all this to do with Peter Redgrove? Everything, in fact. Redgrove and Shuttle work within this Goddess and feminist

---

[29] Judy Chicago, lecture, 1980, in Corrine Robbins: *The Pluralist Era: American Art 1968-1981*, Harper & Row, New York 1984, 53

[30] some of the best books around on the Goddess include: Elinor Gadon: *The Once and Future Goddess*, Aquarian Press 1990; Shirley Nicholson, ed (see bibliography); Barbara G. Walker: *The Woman's Encyclopedia of Myths and Secrets*, Harper & Row, San Francisco, 1983; Esther Harding: *Women's Mysteries*, Rider 1989

tradition. Their *The Wise Wound* was an important contribution to understanding the magico-religious aspects of women's sexuality. Redgrove's poetry comes from the Goddess experience, the 'mother-world', and most of Redgrove's poesie can be seen as Goddess-orientated: from the obvious menstrual eulogy of 'Starlight' to the dragon-wild stormbringing of 'Rainmaking Exercise' and 'The Pale Brows of Lightning'. Kathleen Raine writes: '[Redgrove] is not only a poet of great intelligence, widely and deeply read in many fields; he is alive to what one must call 'the sacred', the abundant generative mystery of Great Dame nature'.

Redgrove exalts women's power. 'To the lover she is the ultimate reality' writes Novalis in his philosophical fragments, as if he's describing the Buddha, or Allah, or Brahma (*Pollen*, 60). In 'The Grand Lunacy' Redgrove writes of the Moon as 'the mansion of the mighty mother' (WNP, 43); in *In the Country of the Skin* the Black Goddess, Teresa, is 'the black lover of animals' (33); while in 'An Egyptian Requiem', Redgrove makes the age-old connections between women, life/ death, the Moon, night, stars and transformation:

Beyond the Hall

Where you eat your heart, is a garden
Which still exists, though men deny it.
This is the starting-point.

As when the Moon dies, and her bones whiten
And crumble into dust of stars, the nightside
Of phenomena where all transforms. (Man, 39)

And in 'The Goging Stool', from *The Mudlark Poems*, Redgrove writes:

The HWCH or Witch. The scribe, the scraper,
The spirit-sculptor of the Mother of All,

Peter Redgrove: Here Comes the Flood

> Mother of Source, the Widow, the One Alone,
> Communicator. All that belonged to that firstness
> Was afterwards derided and denounced but is. (Mud, 19)

In the short story "Ashiepaddle", one of the 'fairy tales' that Redgrove rewrites in a manner that chimes with Angela Carter, Emma Tennant and Sara Maitland, we find the mantra '*Beblack beblack*':

> Being black and clad like the night sky I have become clean too, like a spirit. I am become the very ghost of a black fairy, a piece of invisible night... *Be-black, be-black.* I wear my uterine skin to be near the sources of creation, and they can only see that as darkness. Darkness, and absence, an invisibility running skyclad through the house...[31]

Redgrove speaks of a figure or personage called 'The Witch Who Loves Us' (other figures of his include Faust, the 'scientist of the strange'):

> This person, the Witch Who Loves Us, is a person who is human but is also of the other world, as people of the opposite gender are. I mean, they seem perfectly matter of fact to themselves, but to us they are very mysterious and very energetic and very strange and, of course, stimulate our unconscious minds as they stimulate our sexuality. This Witch Who Loves Us, being a woman, is, of course, privy to what the Student of the Strange regards as magic, that's why she's a witch. And indeed, in rational terms, in accepted terms, if she is the mother of a child, she is the producer, the source of the original magic, which is the creation of persons, without which there will be no magic, science or anything else. (SS)

Redgrove's particular Goddess is Black, called variously Hecate, Isis, Persephone, Medusa, Lilith, Sophia, Kore and Mary Magdalene (BG, xxiii).[32] It is this 'invisible' Goddess that Redgrove exalts in his poetry: '[t]he greatest art depicts these invisibles, the bounty of the goddess,' he writes (BG, 69).

---

[31] "Ashiepaddle", *The One Who Set Out to Study Fear*, 141
[32] Ean Begg: *The Cult of the Black Virgin*, Routledge 1985

We've passed from matriarchy to patriarchy. Now there is something else coming, and who can say what it is? I certainly can't, but it's in the ground. And the ground of it I myself call feminine, yes. I call it black and I call it a goddess. That is to say, it seems to be that the imports growing from the psyche are feminine and are invisible. (PR, 9)

Redgrove develops his Black Goddess in part from Robert Graves, who in the 60s began to write poems to and about this hidden deity who 'represents...a miraculous certitude in love'.[33] Graves never created a systematic mythology of poetry of the Black Goddess, as he did of the White Goddess. He wrote a book on the Black Goddess, but never worked up this hidden, invisible side of his Goddess into something as full-blown as the material in *The White Goddess*. Some of Graves' best poems are Black Goddess poems, such as 'Black', 'The Black Goddess', 'Blaze of Angels', 'The Snapped Thread' and 'Timeless Meeting'. In the amazing poem 'The Snapped Thread' Graves writes in an ecstatic manner of unashamed erotic and spiritual bliss:

> Desire first, by a natural miracle
> united bodies, united hearts, blazed beauty;
> Transcended bodies, transcended hearts.
>
> Two souls now unalterably one
> In whole love always and for ever,
> Soar out of twilight, through upper air,
> Let fall their sensuous burden.[34]

Graves' black mysticism of love is truly ecstatic, for it always emphasizes timelessness, transcendence, bliss and union. Is Redgrove as ecstatic as Graves' late work? Yes, at times he is. In the 1960s, Graves seemed to be burning up with a fierce kind of loving: he spoke of a feverish kind of love which transcended time and space. He wrote of the male-female union as a 'timeless

---

33 Graves: *Mammon and the Black Goddess,* Cassell 1965
34 Graves: *Collected Poems,* Cassell, 1975, 331

now...the *now* of wisdom, the poetic *now*, the *now* of the Black Goddess.'[35] Redgrove is similarly ecstatic. Like Graves, Redgrove believes passionately in the Gnostic/ Neoplatonic idealism of love, where two souls can be 'unalterably one' as Graves puts it. Redgrove says:

> the things that women can give on the personal level by their companionship, their motherhood, and their sexuality are so close to the things that I want to say in poetry. All of my poetry in that sense is love poetry. I'm looking for the missing half, if you like, of the Platonic body, trying to find this in my poetry... This is the love-experiment I am doing. My poetry is one continuous aspiration towards this. (PR, 7)

So the poet searches for his other half, the other soul in the gnostic *syzygy*, that egg which contains two souls like two yolks, the double pelican of alchemy, where two beings initiate and feed each other. This is one of the most deeply desired dreams of Western culture, this two-in-oneness, this mystical union or spiritual marriage, where the King and Queen, brother and sister, sun and moon of alchemy join together.

For the historical origin of this powerful desire for love-union we go back to that mythic figure who, like Orpheus, stands behind so much of Western magic and religion, Plato. In his *Symposium*, Plato wrote:

> Each of us when separated is always looking for his other half; such a nature is prone to love and ready to return love. And when he finds his other half, the pair are lost in an amazement of love and friendship and intimacy...For the entire yearning which each of them has toward the other does not appear to be the desire of intercourse, but of something else which the soul cannot tell and of which she has

---

35 Graves in *Mammon and the Black Goddess*, 147; the Foreword to *Poems About Love*, Cassell 1969, 5

only a dark and doubtful presentiment.[36]

This dream of love lies behind Petrarch's *Canzoniere*, Shakespeare's *Sonnets*, Hardy's novels and poetry, Dante's *Vita Nuova*, John Donne's *Songs*, Goethe's *Werther*, Gide's *Strait Is the Gate* – any number of works of art from the last two millennia. It is Redgrove's theme also, the alchemical wedding. In the apocryphal *Gospel of Thomas* Jesus says

> When you make the two one, and when you make the inner as the outer and the outer as the inner and the above as the below…then shall you enter the Kingdom.[37]

Here, Jesus restates the central tenet of Western magic: *as above, so below*, which we translate in our psychoanalytic era as: *as outside, so inside*.

The Goddess plays a key role in this unification of love. As Redgrove says, '[i]t is not Jesus but his sister that I am interested in, and there is no such Bible' he states (MR). Redgrove is more interested in Shakespeare's sister than the old bard himself.[38] In 'Two of the Books' he compares Shakespeare and the Bible, the two major books of British culture, and of course brings in the Dark Lady, perhaps the most famous Black Goddess in British literature, as well as mentioning Shakespeare's wife (Ark, 149). There are many antecedents of the Black Goddess: Sophia, the Gnostic Goddess of Wisdom; the 'black but comely' Shulamite of the *Song of Songs*; the Black Madonnas found throughout Europe; Lilith, Adam's first lover; Isis; Diana, the Goddess of witches; the Night Mare or succubus; Kali, the Indian Goddess; Hecate; Persephone; Shekinah of Qabbalism; the Sphinx. We find Black

---

36 Plato: *Symposium*, tr Jowett, in Maurice Valency: *In Praise of love: An Introduction to the Love-Poetry of the Renaissance*, Macmillan, New York 1961, 27
37 *The Gospel According to Thomas*, quoted in Nicholson, 49
38 Redgrove says the same thing of Jesus (in MR)

Goddesses in Egyptian religion, Catharism, Arthurian and Grail romance, alchemy, Neoplatonism, witchcraft and the Knights Templar.

There is an element of racism in the term 'blackness'. Peter Redgrove's work is not racist, but images of race occur in his texts, such as the black man in his novel *The God of Glass*. Blackness does not refer to racial origins but to magic, the unconscious and the 'underlife' of things. Redgrove relates the Black Goddess to the original Mother of All, the woman who gave birth to everyone, who lived in Africa thousands of years ago.[39]

Talk of blood ties and blackness can appear dubious, ideologically. Bertrand Russell says that blood ties and hereditary relations can lead to racism and right-wing politics (or reactionary socialism).[40] But if, as the feminist Julia Kristeva notes, meaning is contextual, then in the context of Redgrove's poetry, 'blackness' is magical not political.

Feminism

For Redgrove and Shuttle '[d]arkness is a power. She haunts with power' (from the poem 'Erosion', in *The Hermaphrodite Album*, p.67). *The Hermaphrodite Album* is a collaboration, the title again refers to the longed-for mystic union. The Goddess is seen as a timely counterblast to patriarchy, to 'the strictures of over-masculinized society' as Shuttle puts it (We, 125).

---

[39] see John Groom: "Are we all descended from one woman?", *The Listener*, 27 February 1986, 10-11; Judith Cleeson: Oya: Black Goddess of Africa", in Nicholson, 56,67

[40] Bertrand Russell: *A History of Western Philosophy*, Allen & Unwin, 1971

Redgrove employs some of the notions of the French feminists, which in turn are derived in part from the 'French Freud', Jacques Lacan. Redgrove uses the notion of *jouissance*, for example, the orgasmic nature of writing and texts and reading. He speaks of the 'hysterization of the skin' (Rim, 174). French feminists such as Julia Kristeva celebrate female eroticism, speaking of the 'explosive, blossoming, sane and inexhaustible *jouissance* of the woman'.[41]

It was Luce Irigaray who wrote of all-over female eroticism, which Redgrove agrees with, saying 'woman has sex organs just about everywhere'.[42] For Irigaray, a woman's sex is 'two lips which embrace continually', in which women are parthenogenic, and self-contained, not needing others to pleasure them, because they are pleasuring themselves – continually (in ib., 100). Some feminists, have disagreed with Irigaray's view of female sexuality, because she over-emphasizes eroticism, at the expense of other aspects: '[a]ll that 'is' woman comes to [Irigaray] in the last instances from her anatomical sex, which touches itself all the time. Poor woman.' (M. Plaza, 32)

This sexual over-emphasis can be a problem, and it may be Redgrove's problem too: over-stressing sexuality may, say feminists have negative effects. By reducing people to erotic creatures their potential can be limited. Freud did this by sexualizing everything. In the Freudian view (which is also that of de Sade, Baudelaire, Bataille, etc), the whole world is erotic – caves are vaginas, towers are phalloi. For the intellectuals, sex and death combine, and everything is reducible to sex and death ('birth, copulation and death', said T.S. Eliot, summarizing the cynical, oh-so-clever masculinist view). All this can be severely reductive, squashing the life out of life. Redgrove sometimes evokes sexuality in a similar way to Bataille and Baudelaire. In

---

41 *About Chinese Women*, in Eagleton, 81
42 Luce Irigaray: *Ce sexe qui n'en est pas un*, Minuit, Paris 1977, in Marks & Courtivron, eds, 103

The Duct Redgrove writes of orgasm and death: '[t]he spasm is a momentary incursion into the realm of death... Coitus consists of two people hurling themselves into death but with the ability to return, to live and to remember.' (*The Cyclopean Mistress*, 107)

Redgrove at times goes along with feminists in preaching the sexual superiority of women, of the clitoris, the multi-orgasmic capabilities of women. Women's experiences are 'arguably more deeply actual and rooted in this physical world than any man can attain' he says with Shuttle in *The Wise Wound* (25). Shuttle and Redgrove includes a 'get out clause' here, by using the word 'arguably', otherwise the emphasis on the superiority of women's experience against man's is difficult to defend. The trouble with comparing male and female sensuality is that women's sensuality is usually defined *in opposition to* men's sensuality, and in terms of heterosexuality. Hélène Cixous shows how limiting it is to speak in terms of 'woman' and 'man'.[43] Cixous' Derridean analysis reveals how duality upholds the patriarchal status quo. By stressing the sexual superiority of women, feminists acknowledge male sexuality as the only alternative, as the 'guide' by which to judge female sexuality. Sexual stereotypes are thus endorsed. Instead of men and women we may get reductions to the clitoris and penis. But lovemaking is more than genitals. People are more than that. Sex is more than the rubbing together of penis and clitoris. It may be better to speak of *difference,* as Monique Wittig and Bonnie Zimmerman suggest (in Munt, 3-6).

The emphasis on sexual issues can obscure other crucial issues: of race, of power relations, of enculturation, of labour, of class, of ideology, etc. In Peter Redgrove's poetry we find a lot of sex, and a lot of genitals. For example: 'her cunt gave off a round heat that was in itself a dream.' (CIT, 59) In 'Love's Journeys' we hear of the 'Duchess of Cunt' (Dr, 65: 'the | Duchess of Cunt was waiting | to award me my | school prize of sex- | instruction

---

[43] Hélène Cixous: *Le jeune née*, UGE, Paris 1975, in ib., 90f

booklets'), while in *The Terrors of Dr Treviles* the 'University of Cornwall' is called 'An Cuntellow' (46). Redgrove focuses on sexuality, because for him being alive is itself erotic: his relation with the world is erotic, just as his poems can be seen as 'acts of love'.[44] Eroticism may be his way in to life, a key to life, as well as an expression, as an act, of life. As he writes in his "Rimbaud My Virgil": '[s]ex is a language adequate to express its intensity with its camaraderie an erotic vision of the world – this is the vocation Rimbaud calls us to' (Rim, 177).

Redgrove advocates a multilayered relation to life, hating the reductionist patriarchal view of pornography that sees women as mere 'cunt', and their only function is to be fucked. This is the view of women detested by anti-porn feminists such as Andrea Dworkin, Susan Griffin, Mary Daly and Elizabeth Carola, who wrote: 'the basic male fantasy of Woman as Wholly Sexual Object Whose Purpose is To Be Fucked'.[45]

Redgrove himself is somewhere in the middle ground, somewhere between masculinism and feminism, between pornography and poetry. He says: 'I tend to fall between two stools. I become unpopular with feminists and slightly unpopular with masculinists. I think I may write primarily for women of intelligence and sexuality, who know sexuality is funny as well as spiritual.' (Laz) For Redgrove, the link between poetry and feminism is that poetry (or any creative enterprise) is the activity that can realize the full potential of feminism. Art/ poetry/ creativity brings alive concerns such as feminism. It is a politics of creativity, firmly founded in the imagination and creative potential. He says: 'this magic of inspiration... I'm saying is a common human quality and the redeemer in Jungian terms, is what the women's movement is offering us in the poetry anthologies. Not poetry as an icon to be worshipped but to be participated in to rouse one's own poetry. What could be better?'

---
44 letter to me, 19 May 1993
45 in Gail Chester, 169

(MR). Here, again, Redgrove states his belief, held by other artists and writers, that art can have a healing, therapeutic, nurturing power.

Dualist terms, gender stereotypes, and the language of pornography sometimes occur in Redgrove's work. Some may see his erotic poetry and prose as erotica, others may see it as pornography. For feminists, the erotica/ pornography debate is out-of-date, and misses the point. For anti-censorship feminists, there must be no censorship of any words, whether they be the 'four-letter' words Lawrence employed in *Lady Chatterley's Lover* – *fuck, cunt, shit* – or the terms of extreme politics: fascism, Nazi, anti-semitism, terrorism, racism. The French feminists are wary of using terms such as 'woman', 'feminine' and 'women'. For example, Alice Jardine says that the term 'woman' is really a 'writing-effect'.[46] Dale Spender calls language 'man-made',[47] while Cixous hates the term 'feminine'.[48] Mary Daly has tried to counter patriarchal language by creating one of her own, as has Barbara G. Walker.[49] Other feminists have questioned the notion of a conspiracy of 'man-made language', of language made and policed by men.

In French feminism the text is primary, and a text can be 'feminine' regardless of who creates it. For Hélène Cixous a man can write a 'feminine' text (such as Jean Genet). However, according to Cixous, there are only one or two truly 'feminine' texts (she mentions Colette, Duras and Genet). Redgrove's poetry moves towards the 'feminine', rejoicing in evoking the pleasure (*jouissance*) of the text.

---

46 Alice Jardine: *Gynesis: Configurations of Women and Modernity*, Cornell University Press, Ithaca 1985
47 Dale Spender: *Man-Made Language,* Routledge & Kegan Paul 1985, 12f
48 Hélène Cixous: "The Laugh of the Medusa", *Signs,* Summer 1976, in Marks,253f;
49 see Mary Daly: *Pure Lust: Elemental Feminist Philosophy*, Women's Press 1984, and her *Webster's First New Intergalactic Wickedary of the English Language,* Beacon Press, Boston, 1987; Barbara G. Walker, op.cit.

Peter Redgrove: Here Comes the Flood

The notion of a conspiracy of men controlling women throughout history is rejected by some feminists as hopelessly simplistic, as well as inaccurate. It is too simple to claim that men stole women's power thousands of years ago and have made all the mistakes ever since. There is so much to attack and redress, though. Redgrove and Shuttle have done their bit by writing *The Wise Wound*, which have helped to uncover the taboo-driven disinformation that patriarchy has heaped upon menstruation and women's mysteries.

'We're stormy,' says Hélène Cixous,[50] and women are. For some feminists, it is not that women are not actually 'wilder and stranger' than men, in themselves, rather, women's *cultural space* is wilder and stranger. The *female* 'wild zone', to use Elaine Showalter's useful term, is much wilder and stranger than the *male* 'wild zone'. The female 'wild zone' is still largely unknown. Or rather, still largely unrepresented in patriarchal culture, if indeed it is possible to represent it in patriarchal culture. We know about the male 'wild zone' – it's the stuff of legend, of hunting, of violence, brotherhoods, initiations, etc.[51] The female 'wild zone' is that moon-place/ womb-space of hysteria, menstrual madness, blood mysteries, women's adventures. The 'wild zone' is a cultural more than a biological space; that is, things experienced there are beyond established male culture, and a new language has to be invented to describe experiences in the female 'wild zone'.

Arguments based on biology or essentialism are problematic. The key point of French feminism is that women are not born, one *becomes* a woman, as Simone de Beauvoir put it (Marks, 152). Or as Sheila Jeffreys writes: '[e]very woman grows up in a hetero-patriarchal world' (in Gail Chester, 139). Cultural theory feminists might be critical of Redgrove's essentialist views of 'woman'. A.S.

---
50 H. Cixous, op.cit., p.248
51 Elaine Showalter: "Feminist Criticism in the Wilderness", in Showalter, ed: *The New Feminist Criticism*, Virago 1986, 262-3

Byatt wrote of the 'insistent anthropomorphism' in Redgrove's views. At the same time though, body-awareness is crucial. French feminists such as Madeleine Gagnon write that '[a]ll we have to do is let the body flow, from the inside' (in E. Marks, 180). You'll see the body flooding throughout Redgrove's poems.

Redgrove's sexual texts have the openness – of style and form – of feminist erotica, the sort that is cited by anti-censorship feminists as an example of 'liberated', sexual expression, while the anti-porn feminists might say feminist erotica is really pornography. Susan Griffin is anti-porn but she writes about sex; she has written about rape and male violence from a radical feminist perspective, but has also written powerfully of lesbian eroticism:

> ...my most profound longings and desires, for intimacy, to know, to touch and be inside the body and soul of another, becoming and separating from, devouring and being devoured, that wild, large, amazing, frightening territory of lovemaking belongs for me not with men, but with women.[52]

Redgrove and Shuttle, in *The Wise Wound*, used ancient myths in their analysis of menstrual taboos. But most of the myths are patriarchal. For cultural feminists, where the text is primary, not the author, even if all the authors of all ancient mythologies were female, most of the texts would *still* be patriarchal – in their language, attitudes, values, ideas, taboos and feelings. Shuttle's and Redgrove's goal was to investigate the taboos that have grown up around menstruation, and to use the mythologies as corroborative illustrations of their thesis. But patriarchy is embedded so deeply into language and culture that it is nearly impossible to clear away the disinformation and extract an authentic 'feminine' view from it. Yet the 'feminine' is there, for those who can see it.

There is something in women way beyond men's grasp, some

---
[52] *Viyella*, in Laura Chester, ed: *Deep Down*, 326.

feminists claim. As Xavière Gauthier wrote:

> witches [women] are bursting; their entire bodies are desire; their gestures are caresses; their smell, taste, hearing are all sensual. Their pleasure is so violent, so transgressive, so open, so fatal, that men have not yet recovered. (in Marks, 201)

You might say that Redgrove's work is an attempt to set in writing some of his experiences of this violent, transgressive, multi-sensual and open *jouissance*. This, for instance, Part IV, 'Wardrobe Lady', from 'Six Odes':

> She wears the long series of wonder-awakening dresses,
> She wears the fishskin cloak,
> She wears the gown with the constellations slashed into its dark
>   lining,
> She undresses out of the night sky, each night of the year a different
>   sky,
> She wears altitude dresses and vertigo dresses,
> She plucks open the long staircase at the neck with the big buttons of
>   bird-skulls in the white dress of sow-thistle.
> (SP, 83)

'Redgrove has a tendency to mythologize women to such an extent that he is in danger of placing them on another equally repressive pedestal' writes Mog Ruth. Redgrove says that '[a] religion, any religion worth its name, has to have women in it. Because half the world is' (Hud, 400) Redgrove adores women, but that very adoration can have sexist implications. Goddess worship, for instance, is sexist, defining gender roles and setting out power relations clearly. Goddess worship says men will act like this, and women like that, and, further, it is usually ruthlessly heterosexual. The 'covens' in witchcraft are made up of six men, six women and presiding priest/ess – witchcraft rituals are as sexist and stereotypical as Christianity).[53]

If there is sexism and anti-feminism in Redgrove's works, it's

---

[53] see Mary Daly: *Beyond God the Father*, Women's Press, 1985

not there by intention, it's part of just about *all texts everywhere*. A good deal of *The Wise Wound* is given over to a history of how women have been oppressed – in the mass murder of the witches in the Middle Ages which Shuttle and Redgrove call 'nine million menstrual murders'. *The Wise Wound*, Redgrove says, is about

> the way the masculine non-menstruating spirit prevents women from achieving their own visionary riches by shutting them into a hell of disinformation and stealing the one half of their sexuality – the tabooed menstrual half. (Rim, 174)

Shuttle and Redgrove's menstrual text is dedicated to the creation of a menstrual zone. In *The Guest Father*, Redgrove describes the various aspects of the menstrual cycle, and how his lover's (Penelope Shuttle's) menstrual cycle creates experiences in himself:

> I dream into my wife's menstrual cycle, which is a kind of household weather, and I have dreams which relate to the events of her cycle-day. I dream of treasures put away carefully at the receding threshold of her menstruation, as the tide of blood ebbs; of wonderful rounded treasures at her ovulation: globes, bubbles, fruit, round tables; of terrible deaths at her late luteal phase, when the ovum is breaking up and giving off its last energies, and yet the pregnancy hormone, progesterone, is at peak, potential pregnancy fighting its opposite; of electricity and fire during her advancing premenstrual threshold; of blood and life and mental fertility during her bleeding. (GF, 29)

In 'Valentine' Redgrove evokes this menstrual/ ovular space, where everyday events such as a bath merge with lovemaking and the 'underworld' of existence (Powys' 'underlife') here embodied in the wonders of plumbing:

> Ovulating on St. Valentine's Day.
> She is odorous and voluptuous after her bath.

> With a fine fuzz like a peach. Her water
> Gurgles away into the underground chambers and great shrines
>
> Which it has adorned through her life with her perfumes.
> She who quests is the quest's fulfilment. (Lab, 36)

Shuttle's and Redgrove's menstrual zone is the female 'wild zone'. So feminists speak of experiences beyond male control: pregnancy, childbirth, female orgasm, *jouissance*. Julia Kristeva writes:

> If a woman cannot be part of the temporal symbolic order except by identifying with the father, it is clear that as soon as she shows any sign of that which, in herself, escapes such identification and acts differently, resembling the dream of the maternal body, she evolves into this 'truth' in question. It is thus that female specificity defines itself in patrilinear society: woman is a specialist in the unconscious, a witch, a bacchanalian, taking her jouissance in an anti-Apollonian, Dionysian orgy.[54]

Like the poet, 'woman' is a shaman, a witch, a magician, moving beyond the symbolic/ oedipal/ patriarchal order; 'the female is the initiatrix' writes Alex Comfort (96). Redgrove concurs with this view of 'woman' as witch, shaman, Goddess: he has written many witchy poems: 'The Witch Who Loves Us', 'The Reason Why Witches Wear Black', 'At the Witch Museum', 'Room of Wax', 'Young Women With the Hair of Witches and No Modesty'. One of Redgrove's more feminist poems is the delicious 'Room of Wax' which replays the stereotypes of witchcraft in a parodic manner:

> The witch pulled the lever and her cellar filled with hot wax,
> The mice, the boxes of nails, the live matches,
> The well-head, the altar and the human sacrifice:
> The girl with the welling heart, and the goat-headed man

---

[54] Julia Kristeva: *About Chinese Women*, in *The Kristeva Reader*, ed Toril Moi, Blackwell 1986, 154

> With dagger dripping on the return-stroke –
> Before they knew it, in a flash-flood
> Of hardening wax of bees, caught for ever in the act.
> (WNP, 88)

In 'Water-Witch, Wood-Witch, Wine-Witch', he writes about making love in a cornfield (Dr, 10-12), an image of maximum fertility, which Lawrence used to such great effect in *The Rainbow*:

> She uncaps jars of venomous honey. I take her by the hips
> And lift her down as from a tree. In the cornfield we make our love
> And as we finish the air is thickly grassed with rain.
>   Who was it
> Who smelt even as she frowned in anger
> Of blueberries and honey, in whose honour
> Corn-lightning played over the horizon?

Victor Burgin, describing Julia Kristeva's philosophy, says that she positions

> the woman in society...in the patriarchal, as perpetually at the boundary, the borderline, the edge, the 'outer limit' – the place where order shades into chaos, light into darkness. This peripheral and ambivalent position allocated to woman, says Kristeva, had led to that familiar division of the field of representation in which women are viewed as either saintly or demonic – according to whether they are seen as bringing the darkness, or as keeping it out.

Saintly woman (the Virgin Mary is a typical example) keeps the amazing energy of the female wild zone out of men's lives; the demonic woman (Mary Magdalene, the *femme fatale*, vampire, 'devil woman') is the one who brings the wildness with her. Patriarchy of course prefers bland, mute, passive door-stops in women. For Redgrove, the virgin/ whore, bad woman/ good woman configuration has a menstrual dimension. For him, a witch is a woman in tune with her menstrual cycle. Society, he says, elevates the ovulatory aspect of things – the mother, the passive nurturer (the Virgin Mary is the archetype), but denigrates and denies the menstrual woman, the witch, the 'witchy' woman who becomes objectified as a whore, because she uses transformative, non-procreative sex (i.e., sex during menstruation). The virgin/ whore or mother/ lover duality is found throughout Western culture – in the Virgin Mary/ Mary Magdalene, or in Eve/Lilith, or in the two aspects of Aphrodite.[55]

Mr Redgrove's Goddess has a cosmic dimension. She becomes identified with the fundamental processes of life itself, she is space and time, says Joseph Campbell, while Erich Neumann depicts her as the 'Great Round' into which everyone goes at death.[56] One is reminded of those tumuli and prehistoric tombs where bones were reddened with ochre at burial, perhaps relating to menstrual blood, but certainly relating to the blood of life.[57] There are many prehistoric sites in Cornwall, particularly in the West Penwith peninsula, and this aspect of the Cornish landscape – the massive sepulchral nature of the stones and the granite – finds its way into Redgrove's work (the stone circles are wonderful – Merry Maidens, Tregeseal, and the great Boscawen-Ûn, while the *fogous* or underground tunnels are superbly uterine and Redgrovean).

Curled up in the foetal position, death becomes a rebirth in a different kind of womb, a stone womb. Poets have long made the links between womb and tomb, which is another manifestation of the masculine association of sex and death. In Redgrove's poetics, the menstruating woman is among the most powerful of living beings, and makes clear the mythopoeic continuum of sex, death, rebirth and transformation. The film director Michelangelo

---

55 see Sarah Lucia Hoagland & Julia Penelope, eds: *For Lesbians Only: A separatist anthology,* Onlywomen press 1988; Marina Warner: *Monuments and Maidens,* Weidenfeld & Nicholson 1985

56 Joseph Campbell: *Power,* 167; Erich Neumann: *The Great Mother,* Princeton University Press, New Jersey 1972

57 see Gimbutas; also Monica Sjöo & Barbara Mor: *The Great Cosmic Mother,* Harper & Row, San Francisco, 1987

Antonioni (of *Blow Up* fame) said that being with women makes life richer and deeper somehow: 'I especially love women... Through the psychology of women everything becomes more poignant'.[58] Redgrove writes, in 'Among the Whips and the Mud Baths': '[h]er power makes me see things, I mean her personality' (SP, 137), while in 'A Word' he muses: '[w]omen offer mastery/ Of night' (Man, 89).

For Redgrove, the best thing men can do is to live in mytho/ poetico/ synæsthetic/ multi-tactile relationship with women. Men must live with women, he says in his poetry and in his non-fiction. It is the same with D.H. Lawrence, and Robert Graves, and any number of writers. Lawrence was always going on about 'getting into touch' with life, and this usually meant heterosexual relationships, as he wrote in *Morality and the Novel*: 'the great relationship, for humanity, will always be the relation between men and women' (*Phoenix*, 180).

---

58 Antonioni, in Sam Rohdie: *Antonioni*, British Film Institute 1990, 183

Five

Sex Magic, Sex Alchemy, Sex Yoga

Menstrual Sex

When the woman is menstruating, lovemaking can be visionary and extraordinary, says Redgrove. This is what everyone's interested in, he says: 'that is, a kind of sexuality which is transformative and not for reproduction'.[59] This transformative sex is hated by the church and tabooed by society, even as society is fascinated by it. Witches cultivate the energies released during menstruation, says Redgrove, and he creates a magic, an alchemy, a yoga, a religion out of sex. In an interview, Redgrove gets visionary: 'I would like the whole of Britain to become an enormous Moon College with everybody dreaming their menstrual cycles into knowledge and action.' (PV, 5)

For him, magic itself is erotic – 'true magic is a turn-on' (Rim, 175) – and poetry is erotic, and the erotic is poetic. 'The mutual illumination sex brings us is of a poetic nature' says Penelope Shuttle (We, 127). Sex-poetry-magic-alchemy-yoga-Goddess-feminism-menstruation thus form a continuum which is central to

---
[59] letter to the author, 16 September 1993

Shuttle and Redgrove's life. Everything feeds into everything else. So the orgasmic state becomes creative, and one can ask 'it' things and maybe get back answers. Shuttle explains thus:

> That 'continuity with nature' is what I mean by 'greening the orgasm' and can only be adequately described in poetry...Sex in which my orgasmic potential has been realized, taking Peter with me to match the female capacity, becomes timeless, egoless, and natural. (We, 131)

Redgrove advocates a sexual alchemy based on Tantric, Taoist and Oriental sexual magic, where the man withholds ejaculation and climbs the 'ladder of orgasms' with the woman, who herself is multi-orgasmic, where 'climax can follow climax' (SGH, 49). There are good and bad days for sex in Redgrove's system, and one should use the good days or 'orgasmic windows' (We, 137). The aim is creative union: '[l]ove-making often leads to a creative clarity', he says (ib., 139). He speaks of the 'fluid intoxication between the sexes, a certain chemistry' (CM, 106). Redgrove uses both Taoist and Tantric practices: 'I cannot say which I am closest to, since I have been practising Hatha Yoga for Tantric purposes for nearly a quarter of a century, and consulting the *I Ching* for about that time also. I am closer to Tantra in that I ejaculate, and close to Taoism in that I used the 'Sets of Nine'.'[60]

One chooses the right days in the menstrual cycle: when the egg dies, the potential child is sacrificed (inside the woman), and energy is released and produces transformation and spiritual renewal (ib., 140). This death-and-rebirth cycle is the biological dimension of the Goddess's consort dying and being reborn. The menstrual journey is thus a descent and return, and when the spiritual resurgence occurs, Redgrove says

> it is accompanied with an especial sexual high, which is alchemical and transforms the perceptions, so that everything that falsely appeared dull and 'ordinary' is transformed to the extraordinary,

---
60 letter, 19 May 1993

and makes poems that testify to the joy and the strangeness of descent and return... (We, 140)

You'll see this strangeness and joy in the poems in many of Redgrove's poems: in 'Four Poems of Love and Transition', 'Starlight', 'Entry Fee' and 'A Maze Like Us', for example. These are orgasmic poems, created out of the orgasmic state.

'Entry Fee' combines sex and smell, Cornwall (in the mines) and a startling image – taken from the poet's orgasm – of a swan in a glittering mine:

> When I stroke her arms
> There is a smell of bread;
> Her legs, of lilies.
>
> There are fragrant marshes in her skin
> And there is a pulse in the ground of it.
> The Mine called 'Isyours' is open today
> On payment of a small compliment.
> (FE, 64)

Sometimes Redgrove depicts his beloved as a human figure, but just as frequent are the orgasmic qualities of the natural elements – drenching storms, snaky zigzag lightning strikes, or the perfume rising off a lawn before rain (in 'Word', Man, 89, and WI, 4).

In the *Theatricum Chemicum*, Gerhard Dorn says: '[t]ransform yourselves into living philosophical stones!' (quoted by Jung).[61] And this is precisely what Redgrove tries to do, to transform himself into a living Philosopher's Stone, to become the Holy Grail, the King-Queen alchemical unity. Redgrove gives himself wholly over to the woman, the Goddess. The amazing alchemist Paracelsus (d. 1541) wrote: 'he who would enter the kingdom of God must first enter with his body into his mother and there

---

[61] quoted in C.G. Jung: *Psychology and Religion: East and West*, Routledge & Kegan Paul 1977, 94

die'.[62]

Redgrove, like Paracelsus and the alchemists, advocates a 'dying to' the Goddess, much as Catholic mystics speak of 'dying to' Christ. Redgrove proposes a renaissance of the Goddess symbolized by what he calls an entry into the 'mother-world'. As Paracelsus says, rebirth is essential, but it requires a sacrifice, and it is in the Mother that it occurs. This is a very ancient belief, this return to the Mother figure, the Goddess of All Things. As Marija Gimbutas notes, there is no father figure in prehistory.

Perhaps the reign of the Father Gods is coming to an end, and the Goddess really is returning. For feminists, she has never been away. She has simply been suppressed, like so many things. The Goddess in primaeval times was a 'vast, dark, semiliquid mass of potential energy and matter intermixed' writes Barbara G. Walker.[63] Redgrove taps into this primaeval energy when he is in the post-orgasmic trance, and expresses it in poems such as 'Orgasm', 'The Brilliance', 'Silver Women' and 'Her Shirt Open'. In the novel *The Glass Cottage* the Black Goddess is a 'lady black as the night' (25). And in the poems about mud-bathing, the Goddess is the vast lake of mud in the estuary, the Earth as Black Goddess.

> Foreglow and encounter with P yesterday, her body like a shaking star following the streaming before and after the 'new forest' visited at Redruth – the intercourse a nexus of these currents, a vortex of them as though first the levels were breached by making love to her body, and then the oblation of my semen and my fluttering shirt, the sheet of electricity of my upper-chest and my whole thorax. (GF, 25)

For Redgrove, menstrual sex is the way in to the 'mother-world' when all the senses are acutely and gloriously opened.

---

62 Paracelsus, quoted in Mircea Eliade: *The Forge and the Crucible*, tr Stephen Corrin, University of Chicago Press 1978, 154
63 Barbara G. Walker: *The I Ching of the Goddess*, Harper & Row, San Francisco 1986, 1

'Somehow she opens certain doors in the air', he noted in 'The Golden Policeman' (SP, 173). In menstruation, the woman becomes prescient, a prophetess: '[a]t this time of the month/ When you are your own mistress, mistress of visions' he writes in 'On Having No Head' (Ark, 201). And in "The English Yogi", where elemental sex magic meets the English tea party on the lawn, he writes that 'women are able to see into the land and its bedrock mirrors with the aid of their mirror of blood' (CM, 57). This kind of lovemaking has many names in different cultures. Ginette Paris, for example, speaks of the gold and pink coloured sexuality of the Goddess Aphrodite, which is a form of magical sex.[64] (This rose colour appears in Redgrove's 'The Ninety-Two Demons', in that 'iodine harvest', WNP, 97).

Redgrove writes happily of clitoral sex (he has a poem called 'The Feast Under the Clitoris-Tree'). He does not dislike the clitoris, as Lawrence did, writing of the harsh beak of Aphrodite in *The Plumed Serpent*, associating clitoral sex with 'cock-sure', masculine women. In Redgrove, the womb, vulva, labia and clitoris are lovingly depicted, as in this typical description of clitoral eroticism in "Excursions":

> I wear my pentacle ring on this finger because it is the womanly star, it is the applestar lodged on the clitoral finger which brings down star-jelly by maser: when I tickle you, you diffuse beneficent metals, the familiar room transformed by the sleeping body and its perfumes, wheat springing from her bodice of mud. When we touch our substance we stimulate the universe and ourselves simultaneously. All that glows sees. (CM, 76)

In 'Reader', Redgrove describes an Oriental erotic ritual – the exchanging of sexual essences, in this case, a woman exchanging sperm-laden kisses with her dreaming partner:

---

[64] Ginette Paris: *Pagan Meditations: The Worlds of Aphrodite, Artemis and Hestia*, Spring Publications, Dallas, Texas 1986, 26

Peter Redgrove: Here Comes the Flood

> She sips his seed,
> Her harvest, and then kisses him with her mouth glowing with it, he licks
> His lips and grunts that he has just had a marvellous dream, waking
> To find it true... (*Memes*)

Redgrove draws on many traditions of sex magic: on Taoism and Tantrism. He cites writers such as Mantak Chia, van Lysebeth, B.K.S. Iyengar, Ramsdale, Dorfman, Louise Culling and Stephen Chang. These yoga traditions emphasize the Left Hand path, where the male-female forces of *shiva-shakti* and *yin-yang* are united by *kundalini* yoga and breath control; on sexual alchemy, where the 'Great Work' is the sexual transformation of the male-female energies, here termed king and queen or brother and sister; on Hebrew *horasis* and the shekinah of Qabbalism ('pagan *horasis*, spiritual experience by sexual intercourse, a gnostic position' as he puts it in "The Master-thief");[65] on Gnostic Sophia magic; on Crowleyan sex magicke; on Dianism, etc (BG, 124-168). There are many many kinds of sex magic, amply explored by many writers.[66] The first poem of 'Four Poems of Love and Transition' draws on Oriental sex magic: Redgrove folds in the terminology of Taoist sex practice ('pearl', 'jade pavilion'), and Westernizes it:

> Her great thoroughfare,
> Her sunlit valley, from the testes
>
> Pass multitudes of liquid pearl. Her clitoris
> Is a pearl stud on the jade step whereby

---

65 in *The One Who Set Out to Study Fear*, 80
66 Redgrove recommends the following books on sex magic (among others): Stephen T. Chang: *The Tao of Sexuality*, Tao Publishing 1986; Mantak Chia: *Taoist Secrets of Love,* Aurora Press, New York 1984; Louis T. Culling: *A Manual of Sex Magick*, Llewellyn Publications, Saint Paul, Minnesota 1971; Margo Anand: *The Art of Sexual Ecstasy*, Aquarian Press 1990

The jade pavilion is set on fire.
(UR, 37)

In a letter to me, Redgrove explains what is desired in sex magic:

> What one wants to aim for is the 'staircase' with the man controlling his ejaculation and following with mini-climaxes the woman's sequential orgasms until they take each other...One may gently and courteously petition within before sex (this is the sex magick) and watch what happens during or in the afterglow. This is not to be taken as a right or technique, but as sexual prayer.[67]

The goal is this bliss, sometimes called the 'Magickal Child', as opposed to the flesh-and-blood child created during ovulation.

> Complex virtuous acts and deep intercourse, this presence requires them by the natural mesmerism of the sexual act
> as a magical child is present in both simultaneously
> the magical child or field between the partners
> (*The Guest Father*, GF, 26)

A natural, creative, waking dream, in which the lovers can dream the same dream, 'and the most beautiful pictures of places you have visited seem to rise through the skin' ("Greening the Orgasm", 30). 'The proper state of mind is inspiration', Redgrove says (Hud, 385).

For some, this menstrual, magical, transformative sex, where the 'exiled Black Goddess of supersensible eroticism (BG, 166) is brought back into the foreground of life, is sexist, because it defines the roles of each partner all too clearly. Indeed, Redgrove's sex magic is predominantly heterosexual, and makes few plans for other forms of eroticism, apart from masturbation (Roberts, 28). Further, it focuses on sex not love, which annoys

---

[67] letter to the author, 2 September 1992

some people.[68] Also, it does not operate within the spiritual and social contexts of a mainstream religion, which some people may find unsettling.

Actually, Redgrove has created his own religion or cult. All artists do this. The shaman, as anthropologists tell us, is both the god/ creator and the priest/ servant of her/ his cult.[8] Anyway, Redgrove's cult of sex magicke is firmly situated within the traditions of mainstream religion, within age-old occultism and magic – as found in Tantrism, Taoism, Hinduism, Gnosticism, Qabbalism, etc.

Some feminists will like Peter Redgrove's sex magic, because it empowers the woman ('[w]omen are divinities, they are life', said no less an authority than the Buddha).[69] Other feminists will find Redgrove's sex alchemy limiting in its sexual role playing and gender stereotyping. This kind of sex yoga is not alien to certain strands of Catholicism, for instance. Meinrad Craighead, working within the Christian mystical tradition, writes: '[o]ur spirituality should centre on the affirmation of our female sexuality in its seasons of cyclic change.'[70] Many feminists embrace both Christianity and sexuality, both occultism and the body.

Redgrove's alchemy of sex is close to Taoism. Goddess worship is close to Taoism in its worldview (Nicholson, 19). The *Tao Te Ching* speaks of 'knowing the feminine'. The Black Goddess is quite at home in Taoism too, for the *Tao Te Ching* embraces the dark side of the feminine: 'keep to the feminine',

---

68 A letter from Diana Johnston in *Resurgence* (no. 151, 45) criticizes Redgrove's article "Greening the Orgasm" (*Resurgence* no.150, Jan/ Feb 1992) thus: 'crude, insensitive and offensive to women...Redgrove's article is an end-gaining exercise, i.e. climax orientated and concerned only with the multi-orgasmic couple "taking each other"'
69 De La Vallé Poussin: *Bouddhisme: études et matériaux*, Paris, 1898, 144; and see Julius Evola: *The Metaphysics of Sex*, East-West Publications, 1983, 241
70 in Mary Giles, ed: *The Feminist Mystic*, Crossroad, New York, 1986, 79

the *Tao* says, 'keep to the black'.[71] In 'The Idea of Entropy at Maenport Beach', the protagonist learns that '[i]t is quite wrong to be all white always' and remarks 'I shall take great care/ To keep a little black about me somewhere.' (SP, 67) French feminists such as Julia Kristeva have found a different, deeper sexual connection between men and women in Far Eastern countries (see Kristeva's *About Chinese Women*).[72]

Redgrove's holistic view is Taoist, where all things are interlinked, and a spirit pervades everything: this is the Goddess. You can see that Taoist unification of the cosmos in *In the Esplumeor* where, after lovemaking, all number of things are linked by the poetry of orgasm: the house, underground caves, clouds, ghosts, jewels, a herb garden after rain, etc:

> After sex the woman goes about the house, singing. She sets the rose in motion. She sets the house in motion, she is gliding, the rooms revolve round her, she is the centre. We do not go upstairs; the stairs travel downwards at our command under our feet. The smell of a mother's early-morning arms. The perfumes of the bed transmitted about the house by the great gasps and billowings of the blankets in bedmaking. They practised yoga until beauty was present. We both occupied the form of a woman. Her body gave off a sudden potion of scents like a herb-garden in a sudden shower of rain. A woman like a magnetic wave, the crest of her hair. The invisible body which accompanied her. The pocket full of posies: the cave of underground flowers, the perfume of the earth, the underground fairyland. As it travels under our foundations reflecting the clouds above, our house is set in motion around the centre where I penetrate her nature; her body, the house-body filled with our ghost, set into perfumed resonance. The pyrosome of love-fire, wildfire. (CM, 151)

These thoughts are not exclusive to Redgrove. Marge Piercy writes in a poem, 'Rainin' Pumpernickel': '[y]our love comes down rich as the warm spring rain' (in Chester, 124), while Laura

---
71 *Tao Te Ching*, tr D.C. Lau, Penguin, 1963, 83
72 Julia Kristeva: *About Chinese Women*, tr Anita Barrows, Marion Boyars, 1977

Chester writes in a Redgrovean mode: '[y]our pheromone's my one cologne' (ib., 112), and Sue Miller writes of sex thus: '[i]n those early mornings it all tasted of sex after a few moments...The whole room seemed full of our commingled, complicated smells' (ib., 101).

This flowing, perfumed bliss is dependent on the woman – the 'mediatrix' as Redgrove calls her (TLS), the 'mistress of visions' (in 'On Having No Head', Ark, 199). She is the one who 'sets the house in motion'. In 'The Olfactors', in *Abyssophone*, Redgrove writes of the house as a palace of yonis, or vulvas:

> Whatever the home, it is a palace when perfumed.
> Smells deepen the mirrors to corridors of yonis,
> Polished tables to abysmal wells –
> Chin-in-hand like the stars in the long galleries
> Of night we peer over the abysses,
> For we are back in the yoni now, and can prophesy. (A, 14)

Lawrence Durrell became interested in Taoist love magic and made it a theme in his *The Avignon Quintet*. In his book on his meeting with the writer Jolan Chang, author of *The Tao of Love and Sex*, Durrell writes:

> The gratification of the lovers lay on a different plane; by dint of mastering the orgasm one raised love to a higher frequency. One prolonged life, the immortal life which one was in honour to try and realize upon earth...In the love-making of which the Taoist doctrines there could supervene an orgasm without loss of the vital Taoist essence. It was a question not only of conscious practice but of rapport, of attachment – the whole precious transaction was lifted to a new height of intensity which could endure for hours at a time, if necessary, because the two spirits remained enmeshed in each other.[73]

---

[73] Lawrence Durrell: *A Smile In the Mind's Eye,* Wildwood House 1980, 13,18

Peter Redgrove: Here Comes the Flood

Beyond Sex?

No, Peter Redgrove will not go beyond sex. He lives wholly in the body, like D.H. Lawrence. Any worldview/ system/ religion/ poetry/ magic must embrace the body. If it doesn't, it's too abstract, too distanced, too unreal. Redgrove's poetry never loses touch of the body. You won't find much political commentary, sociological analysis, mathematics, traditional philosophy, history, linguist investigations, finance, the media and melodrama in his poetry. For some people, this lack of politics or social commentary might be a deficiency, but Redgrove's real world is a different one from the so-called 'real' world of advertizing, consumerism and global politics. Redgrove's real world is that of apples, bees, clouds, oceans, hands and wombs. If that isn't 'real' enough for some people, they must be on the wrong planet. You might find broadcasting mentioned – but not relating to TV or radio in the way you'd expect – see the idiosyncratic idea in the poem 'Far Star', for example, which says: '[s]he was broadcast into this world via the lady transmitter' (IHS, 36), or the poem 'Waterworks as Broadcasting House' (Wo, 34). Radio is mentioned in Redgrove more than TV not because radio is full of voices in darkness, which so accords with the experience of consuming poetry, but because the notion of radio waves fanning outwards constantly from aerials and passing through the whole world and space fascinates the poet. Television seems to come directly into the home, but radio gives the impression of distance, of travelling from a particular place ('This is London', 'This is Radio Moscow', 'This is the Voice of America', 'This news bulletin comes to you from Radio Prague'). Radio waves have been travelling way beyond the solar system a long time before television. For Redgrove, the world is full of radio waves, and the poet is the shaman who can capture them, as can animals. In "My Shirt of Small Checks", the 'madman' is clearly a modern madman:

> 'Let Broadcasting House declare an amnesty and a ceasefire,' cries the madman, as the Open University flows over his head, 'for there is only noise where there should be silence! My talent,' he cries, 'was to tune into the silence as I wished, to the sea, to the whale-song and dolphin sonar-talk (in which illumination counts for less than transparency!); to the white crests of the sizzling ionosphere; to the moon as it flies overhead pulling babies out of mothers and dying persons out of their own gasping mouths, its strata bowing against strata, like an orchestra of violins; to the endless warm broadcast of the sun that feed us all,' the madman says,. 'Why, as the sun goes down, BBC 2 rises, and passes across the heavens, and sometimes does not set until one o'clock the next morning.' (CM, 19-20)

For Redgrove, all the agony and ecstasy flows from women, from the 'mother-world'. 'The fool is caught in his mother the rain' he writes in "Mood" (CM, 40), and in *In the Country of the Skin* he writes: '[t]here is a shape between her legs which smells of mountains scraping stationary clouds.' (38) Redgrove's magical view of women, love, the feminine and the Goddess is cosmic, and extends, as the quote from *In the Country of the Skin* suggests, to the very farthest reaches of the universe. The Goddess's power expands to clouds, mountains, orchards, underworlds and the stars: '[m]enstruating, the stars are out' he writes in 'Starlight' (FE, 24).

The feminine infuses everything, somewhat in the pantheist tradition, where God and Nature are identical – *Deus sive Natura* in Baruch Spinoza's words.[74] In a similar way, the Tao pervades everything, as does Brahma or Self in Hinduism. Pantheism is found in Eckhart, Dionysius the Areopagite, Boehme, Nicholas of Cusa, and any number of poets. Redgrove's religion of love is closest to Tantrism – Tantrism modulated by Taoism, where Tantric Hinduism is a 'kind of inner-cosmology of individuation' as Alex Comfort puts it (114). Redgrove explores the links

---
74 quoted in Ferguson, 138

between Western (Jungian) psychology and Oriental sex yoga ('Tantriks are... experimental Jungians' says Comfort, 89). In Hindu Tantra, the Goddess Shakti is all-pervasive: '[w]hatever power anything possesses, that is the Goddess' say the Tantric texts.[75] Redgrove was moving in this mystical all-in-one direction in his earliest poetry. In 'The Ferns' he writes: '[a]ll's water' (For, 17). He could be saying 'all's the Goddess', for the mystical identification of the Goddess and the ocean is ancient (feminists such as Monica Sjöo and Barbara Walker speak of the Goddess as a primaeval mass of energy, as we have said).

Redgrove knows it is crucial to cultivate experiences in the 'mother-world', to keep in touch with the feminine, as the *Tao Te Ching* puts it. Redgrove is someone who has tried to feminize himself in the Jungian manner. 'The second birth is through a spiritual mother', says a post-Jungian, Joseph Campbell, echoing the doctrine of the alchemist Paracelsus (quoted above). Diving into the spiritual mother means acknowledging all manner of dark powers, where 'all surfaces become depths'. As he says in *The Alchemical Journal*: 'I knew she was better than beautiful: she was magic' (AJ, no.27).

Whether she's in the stars menstruating, or in the ocean dreaming, or in the clouds releasing 'skin-orgasms', the Goddess is everywhere, like the spirit of the universe, the Tao, or Brahma, or Shakti, or *shekinah*, or Sophia, or Isis. In *Philosopher and Skin*, a recent prose piece, Redgrove writes:

> Not an independent subject confronting an objective, alien world, but rather the so-called subjectivity, the ego or inner sanctum, and nature, and other people, and the whole world, emerge from a common ground, embracing both humans and nature. (EA, 140)

---

75 in Ferguson, 186

Six

Critical Appraisal

It is deeply unfashionable in some circles to be religious, or to say that this 'common ground', or source of all life, is the Goddess. (Although the idea of 'Gaia', the ecological deity which is the Earth's consciousness, is not a new idea, invented by scientists this century, and Sartre's global village of the mid-century is also nothing new).[76] British literary critics, for example, detest such ideas. Most of them revere the grumpy librarian, Philip Larkin, and can't deal with anything wilder.

When Robert Graves and Philip Larkin died around the same time (December, 1985), there was much attention in the press and media about Larkin, but little about Graves. This says it all about the provincial nature of British lit'ry criticism, and criticism in general. It is very conservative. Like the Judaeo-Christian religions, literary criticism defends itself fiercely against attacks from outside with threaten its stability. It takes years for wild talent to be normalized and woven into the fold (such as Rimbaud). Robert Graves is depicted as a charming but bizarre poet, he is regarded as one of those English eccentrics. Philip Larkin, meanwhile, is

---
76 Campbell, *Power*, 179; Sartre, in H.M. Block, op.cit.

beatified. Why? It's obvious: because Larkin flatters the critics' own views of themselves. This is also the reason why there are so few 'great' women poets: because women poets often write of things beyond male critics' experience or beliefs.

So Redgrove, with his magical feminist synæsthesia, doesn't fit in to the British cosy-armchair pipe-and-tea net-curtains TV-soap-opera-news stiff-upper-lip suburban world. 'Peter Redgrove is universally admired but still has an outsider status in relation to the poetic mainstream, which is puzzling' writes Adam Thorpe. Seamus Heaney comments: 'Redgrove's abundance and stamina as a conjuror of strangeness seem to me to be greatly under-admired, yet that has perhaps come about because of the very opulence of his imagination'. Redgrove's is too 'abundant' for the literary establishment, it seems. What would the literary mafia make of this:

> I have the flames
> in my cunt
> and would burn everything
> to get you

This poem, by Lily Pond,[77] blasts away all the sarky, dull, morbid, dusty male British kind of poetry. Using Redgrove's and Shuttle's psychological approach, we can see that Pond's poem is a cry of rage of love in the manner of Sappho stemming from menstrual hysteria, a menstrual mania which tears apart patriarchy and strikes out for the female 'wild zone'. We quote this poem to show that Redgrove's is not the only form of wild poetry around at the moment.

This is what Robert Graves does with Philip Larkin – blasts him away poetically. But Brit lit crits will have none of it, and they cling onto Larkin and his fellow versifiers.

The rage in poets such as Sappho, Adrienne Rich, Lily Pond,

---

77 Lily Pond: 'Ovulation', in Chester, ed, 151

Sylvia Plath, Anna Akhmatova, Louise Labé, Gaspara Stampa, Marie Tsvetayeva, Yü Hsüan-chi, Rabi'a and Chu Shu-chen simply cannot be contained or controlled by men, male critics or patriarchy. Their poetry is too wild, too strange (yet also everyday). Women poets get sidelined because masculinist criticism does not know what to do with them. If we get the impression that most critics are wimpy, grey, bland, white, Anglo-Saxon, middle class males, we are not far wrong. And if the critics themselves are not like this, then most of their criticism is: wimpy, grey, bland, white, Anglo-Saxon, middle class and patriarchal. It is the consensus of criticism.

So poets such as T.S. Eliot, one of the most unerotic of all poets, gets glorified. And Larkin. And Betjeman. And Alvarez. Yuk. Ted Hughes, for example, is canonized by critics because his world-view accords with theirs. He writes in an earthy, violent, muscular, masculine, neo-Jungian and religious fashion, with his Biblical ithyphallic gods crawling through the planet's undergrowth at worm-level, like Herne the Hunter, or the Celtic god Cernunnos, or the Greek Pan. The Goddess is there in Hughes ('[w]ho is this?/ She reveals herself and is veiled' he writes in *Gaudete* (*Selected Poems*, 158). And a late, lengthy exploration of William Shakespeare took in the Goddess: *Shakespeare and the Goddess of Complete Being*. Hughes' view of love veered between delicate spirituality and violent sensuality. In 'Lovesong', he evoked a vicious kind of sex:

> His sucked out her whole past and future or tried to
> He had no other appetite
> She bit him she gnawed him she sucked
> She wanted him complete inside her (ib., 128)

Here the woman is the voracious whore of pornography, a standard stereotype, the woman as the death-bringing gateway to Hell.

Peter Redgrove: Here Comes the Flood

Hughes and Redgrove, like Yeats and Graves, use heaps of shamanism, Western magic and Jungian myth and psychology. But Redgrove is the most feminized Goddess-soaked poet of his generation – beside him other writers of his generation look positively masculinist in the extreme: Hughes, Ballard, Gunn, Amis, Silkin, Porter, MacBeth, Middleton and Hill.

All the 'great' and 'important' names of British poetry – Eliot, Muir, Betjeman, Watkins, R.S. Thomas, Larkin, Davie – they're oh-so clever, and witty, and topical, but, really, of little value. After you've read Rilke or Eluard or Rimbaud, you don't bother reading many British poets. Except the odd one or two. Redgrove is one of those few. We rate Redgrove highly because he is open to perceptions/ insights/ experiences which the poetry establishment consigns to the fringe.

The critical view of Redgrove is mixed. For many he is 'over-ripe', as Edna Longley puts it. For Alan Jenkins, Redgrove's poems 'occasionally have recourse to a fairly tired repertoire of post-Romantic props, but some of these – spiders, dew, silk... have the charge of personal obsession.'

Critics have acknowledged Redgrove's ability to create magic. 'Redgrove's language can light up the page' wrote Angela Carter. 'His technical brilliance as a poet' writes Peter Finch, 'is unquestioned. Rich language embedded with unexpected images. Form. Control.' 'Redgrove's poetry is a reinvigoration of vision and of language,' writes Malcolm Hebron, 'He is a master at investing the stalest and most commonplace expression with new meaning'. Many critics have praised Redgrove's wide-ranging perception, which takes in so much of the world. Peter Forbes writes: '[e]verything goes into the alchemical Hoover of Redgrove's gaze and comes out looking like the first day of Creation.' Peter Reading wrote in *The Sunday Times*: 'Paul Klee spoke of taking a line for a walk: Peter Redgrove drags ideas on orienteering sprees.' Some critics, such as Phil Hine and Mog

Ruth, are very enthusiastic about Redgrove's theory of magic and extra-sensuous perception, especially as espoused in *The Black Goddess and the Sixth Sense*. Other critics aren't so convinced. Jay Ramsay writes:

> I had some reservations, mostly around his definition of magic, and his exoneration of 'black' magic which I found inadequate and potentially lethal in its failure to recognise the hazards of possession and inflooding, however psychologically aware we may believe ourselves to be. We need to ask who or what is this serving? That is Parsifal's question in the Grail story and it seems to me relevant here. There is danger and there is limitation – we can get stuck at the level of the archetypal without realizing that in fact we need to go further. Where to? To a magic that insists on its own transparency, and its alignment to what is higher – to what goes beyond it.

Poets know that *writing of love* is like *loving itself,* that *describing sex is like having sex.* Otherwise, why did Petrarch write 366 sonnets and *canzones* to his beloved Laura? Or why did Robert Graves fill his *Collected Poems 1975* with hundreds of love poems? Or why did Shakespeare write 154 sonnets? This is the *jouissance* of the text. Writing becomes sex, poetry and love fuse, and the transformative magic of art is as real as the touch of one's lover in the darkness of a room, or salt on one's lips from the sea, or the sudden brilliance of the sun bursting from behind a cloud. Redgrove has shown that poetry is physical, that words are concrete, real things that affect us physiologically as well as emotionally and spiritually. In this he develops the Symbolist thought of Rimbaud, Verlaine, Mallarmé and Valéry, but it is very useful for us to be reminded that poetry is physical, real, flesh-and-blood magic as well as soaringly spiritual.

Bibliography

All books published in London, England, unless otherwise stated.
Abbreviations appear after each entry

Peter Redgrove: Poetry

The Collector and Other Poems, Routledge & Kegan Paul, London, 1960
The Nature of Cold Weather and Other Poems, Routledge and Kegan Paul, London, 1961 [NCW]
At the White Monument and Other Poems, Routledge & Kegan Paul, London, 1963 [WM]
The God-Trap, Turret Books, London, 1966
The Force and Other Poems, Routledge & Kegan Paul, London, 1966 [For]
The Sermon, Poet & Printer, London, 1966
Work in Progress, Poet & Printer, London, 1969
Penguin Modern Poets 11 (with D.M. Black & D.M. Thomas), Penguin, 1968
The Mother, the Daughter and the Sighing Bridge, Sycamore Press, 1970
The Bedside Clock, Sycamore Press, London, 1971
Three Pieces For Voices, Poet and Printer, 1972
Dr Faust's Sea-Spiral Spirit and Other Poems, Routledge & Kegan Paul, London, 1972 [Dr]

In the Country of the Skin: A Radio Script, Peter Redgrove, Falmouth, 1973 [ICS]

Words, Words Press, 1974

Sons of My Skin: Redgrove's Selected Poems 1954-1974, ed. M. Peel, Routledge & Kegan Paul, London, 1975

From Every Chink of the Ark and other new poems, Routledge & Kegan Paul, London, 1977 [Ark]

Skull Event, Sceptre Press, Knotting, 1977

Ten poems, Words Press, 1977

The Fortifiers, the Vitrifiers and the Witches, Sceptre Press, 1977

Happiness, Priapus, 1978

The White, Night-Flying Moths Called Souls, Sceptre Press, Knotting, 1978

The Weddings at Nether Powers and other new poems, Routledge & Kegan Paul, London, 1979 [WNP]

The Apple-Broadcast and other new poems, Routledge & Kegan Paul, London, 1981 [AB]

Martyr of the Hives, in *Best Radio Plays of 1980*, Eyre Methuen, London, 1981

Cornwall in Verse, ed. P. Redgrove, Secker & Warburg, London, 1982

The Working of Water, Taxus Press, Durham, 1984 [WW]

The Man Named East and other new poems, Routledge & Kegan Paul, London, 1985 [Man]

The Mudlark Poems and Grand Buveur, Rivelin Grapheme Press, 1986 [Mud]

Explanation of Two Visions: Poems, Sixth Chamber Press, 1986

In the Hall of the Saurians, Secker & Warburg, London, 1987 [IHS]

Poems 1954-1987, Penguin, London, 1989 [Sel]

The First Earthquake, Secker & Warburg, London, 1989 [FE]

Dressed As For a Tarot Pack, Taxus, Exeter, 1990 [Tar]

Under the Reservoir, Secker & Warburg, London, 1992 [UR]

The Laborators, Stride, Exeter, 1993 [Lab]

My Father's Trapdoors, Cape, London, 1994

Abyssophone, Stride, Exeter, 1995

Sex-Magic-Poetry-Cornwall: A Flood of Poems, ed. and essay by J. Robinson, Crescent Moon, 1994

Assembling a Ghost, Cape, London, 1996

The Best of Peter Redgrove's Poetry: The Book of Wonders, ed. J. Robinson, Cres-cent Moon, 1996

What the Black Mirror Saw, Stride, Exeter, 1997

Orchard End, Stride, Exeter, 1997
Selected Poems, Cape, London, 1999
From the Virgil Caverns, Cape, London, 2002
Sheen, Stride, Exeter, 2003
A Speaker For the Silver Goddess, Stride, Exeter, 2006
The Harper, Jonathan Cape, London, 2006

Peter Redgrove: Prose

In the Country of the Skin, Routledge & Kegan Paul, London, 1973/ Stride, Exeter, 2006
Miss Carstairs Dressed For Blooding and Other Plays, Boyars, London, 1976
The God of Glass: A Morality, Routledge & Kegan Paul, London, 1979/ Stride, Exeter, 2006
The Sleep of the Great Hypnotist: The Life and Death and Life After Death of a Modern Magician, Routledge & Kegan Paul, London, 1979/ Stride, Exeter, 2006
The Beekeepers, Routledge & Kegan Paul, London, 1980/ Stride, Exeter, 2006
Martyr of the Hives, in *Best Radio Plays of 1980,* BBC Publications, London, 1981
The Facilitators or, Madam Hole-in-the-Day, Routledge & Kegan Paul, London, 1982/ Stride, Exeter, 2006
Time For the Cat-Scene in Words, The New Literary Forum, 5, Oct 1985, 6, Nov, 1985
The One Who Set Out to Study Fear, Bloomsbury, London, 1989
"The Cyclopean Mistress – Short Fiction, or Prose Poem? - An Argument in Progress", 1990, unpublished
An Alchemical Journal, 1990, unpublished MS, and in *The Cyclopean Mistress* [A]
A Crystal of Industrial Time, Manhattan Review, 1990, 59-62 [CIT]
*Eight Alcameo*s, *Sulfur* (29), Winter, 1991-92, 133-140 [EA]
"The Cyclopean Mistress", "Greedy Green", "Strong Sugar", "The Model", "Cold University" [prose pieces], *Proposition* (4), 1991 [Pro]
"Introducing Peter Redgrove", *Poetry USA,* 24, 1992

Peter Redgrove: Here Comes the Flood

The Cyclopean Mistress: Selected Short Fiction 1960-1990, Bloodaxe Books, Newcastle, 1993 [CM]

Peter Redgrove: Non-fiction

"Interview with Peter Redgrove", *Hudson Review,* 28, 3, Autumn, 1975 [Hud]
"A Poet in Teaching: A Personal Account", *New Universities Quarterly,* Spring, 1980
"The Dialogue of Gender: Penelope Shuttle and Peter Redgrove", in M. Wandor, ed. *On Gender and Writing*, Pandora, London, 1983
"Scientist of the Strange: An Interview with Peter Redgrove", P. Fried, *Manhattan Review*, 3, 1, Summer, 1983 [SS]
"Lazarus and the Visionary Truth: An Interview with Peter Redgrove", C. Ashcroft, *Arrows* (Sheffield), 1984 [Laz]
"May Day at Padstow", "Effigy Burning", "Men, Menstruation and the Moon", in C. Rawlence, ed. *About Time*, Cape, London, 1985
"Peter Redgrove: The Science of the Subjective" [interview], *Poetry Review*, June, 1987, 4-10 [PR]
The Black Goddess and the Sixth Sense, Bloomsbury, London, 1987 [BG]
"On *The Apple Broadcast*", in J. Barker, ed. *Thirty Years of the Poetry Book Society 1956-1986,* Hutchinson, London, 1988, 166-7
"Work and Incubation: A Sketch of My Method of Writing", July, 1988, unpublished MS [WI]
[On poetry, women and feminism], article in *Times Literary Supplement*, 3-9 June, 1988 [TLS]
"Rimbaud My Virgil", *Sulfur* (30), Spring, 1992, 172-178
"Greening the Orgasm", *Resurgence* (150), Jan/ Feb, 1992, 30-33 [GO]
"Sisters on the sexual picket line [review of Chris Knight's *Blood Relations*]", *Times Literary Supplement*, 7 February, 1992, 21
"Interview with Peter Redgrove", *Pagan Voice*, 6, May, 1992, 4-5
"From *The Guest Father*", *Sulfur*, 34, Spring, 1994, 19-29
'Reader', in *Memes*, 9, April 1994, 41
The Colour of Radio: Essays and Interviews, ed. N. Roberts, Stride, Exeter, 2006

Peter Redgrove: Here Comes the Flood

Peter Redgrove with Penelope Shuttle

The Hermaphrodite Album, Fuller d'Arch Smith, 1973
The Terrors of Dr Treviles: A Romance, Routledge & Kegan Paul, London, 1976/ Stride, Exeter, 2006
The Glass Cottage, Routledge & Kegan Paul, London, 1976/ Stride, Exeter, 2006
The Wise Wound: Menstruation and Everywoman, Paladin, London, 1986
The Menstrual Mandala, 1991, unpublished MS
"Peter Redgrove and Penelope Shuttle" [interview] *We Two: Couples talk about living, loving and working partnerships for the 90s,* ed. R. Housden & C. Goodchild, Aquarian Press/ Thorsons, 1992
"How We Met", interview by E. Oxford, *The Independent on Sunday,* 16 August, 1992, 61
Alchemy For Women, Rider, London, 1995 [AFW]

Others

Geoffrey Ashe: *Discovering the Goddess,* Crescent Moon 1994
Cliff Ashcroft: "The Novels of Peter Redgrove", *Arrows,* Sheffield, 1984
— "A Study of the Poetry of Peter Redgrove with Particular Reference to His Nine Major Volumes, 1959-1985", thesis, *Sheffield University 1989*
Charles Baudelaire: *Oeuvres Complètes,* Bibliothèque de la Pléiade, Gallimard, Paris 1975
—*Artificial Paradises,* Herder & Herder, New York 1971
Ean Begg: [review of *The Black Goddess*], *Harvest,* 188-9
Ernst Benz: *The Mystical Sources of German Romantic Philosophy,* tr B. Reynolds & E. Paul, Pickwick, Allison Park 1983
Harold Bloom, ed: *Arthur Rimbaud,* Chelsea House Publishers, New York 1988
Martin Booth: *British Poetry 1964-1984: Driving Through the Barricades,* Routledge & Kegan Paul, 1985
Victor Burgin: "Geometry and Abjection", in John Fletcher and Andrew Benjamin, eds, 115-6
Jerome Burne: "Going round in circles in search of a memory", *The Observer,* 20 March 1994, 27

A.S. Byatt: "Control of the life-sources", *Times Literary Supplement*, 12-18 August 1988, 890
Joseph Campbell: *The Power of Myth*, with Bill Moyers, ed. Betty Flowers, Doubleday, New York 1988
Angela Carter: *Evening Standard*, 13 April 1989
Gail Chester & Juliene Dickey, eds: *Feminism and Censorship: The Current Debate*, Prism Press, Bridport, Dorset 1988
Laura Chester, ed: *Deep Down: New Sensual Writing by Women*, Faber 1988
Henri Clemens Birven: *Novalis, Magus der Romantik*, Schwab, Büdingen 1959
Alex Comfort: *I and That*, Beazley 1979
Erica Duncan: "Peter Redgrove and Penelope Shuttle: The Joys and Perils of Collaboration", *Book Forum*, vol. VII, no.4, 1986
Mary Eagleton, ed: *Feminist Literary Criticism*, Longman 1991
Terry Eagleton: "Rituals of the Mind", *The Literary Review*, August 1987
H.W. Fawkner: *The Ecstatic World of John Cowper Powys*, Associated University Presses, Cranbury, New Jersey 1986
John Ferguson: *An Illustrated Encyclopaedia of Mysticism*, Thames & Hudson 1976
Peter Finch: [review of *Dressed As For a Tarot Pack*], *New Welsh Review*, Winter 1990
John Fletcher & Andrew Benjamin, ed; *Abjection, Melancholia and Love: the Work of Julia Kristeva*, Routledge 1990
Jack Foley: "Introducing Peter Redgrove", *Poetry USA*, (24), 1992, Oakland, California
Peter Forbes: [review of *The First Earthquake*], *The Listener*, 18 January 1990
R. Garfitt, ed: *Poetry Review*, 71-72, 1981
Alicen Geddes: [review of *Dressed As For a Tarot Pack*], *Topical Books*, Winter 1990
Marija Gimbutas: *The Language of the Goddess*, Thames & Hudson 1989
Michael Hamburger: *Reason and Energy: Studies in German Literature*, Weidenfeld & Nicolson 1970
Thomas Hardy: *The Life of Thomas Hardy*, Macmillan 1967
Seamus Heaney: *Oxford Lectures*, 1990
Malcolm Hebron: [review of *The First Earthquake*], *Oxford Poetry*, 1989
Martin A. Hibbert: "Scents and Super-Sense [review of *The Laborators*]", *Memes*, 8, 1993, 30-31

Phil Hine: [review of *The Black Goddess*], *Pagan News*, January 1989
Ted Hughes: *Selected Poems 1957-1981*, Faber 1982
— *Crow*, Faber 1974
— *Poetry in the Making*, Faber 1969
— *Shakespeare and the Goddess of Complete Being*, Faber 1992
Michael Hulse: [review of *Poems 1954-1987, The First Earthquake* and *The Black Goddess*], *Acumen*, Winter 1990
Luce Irigaray: *The Irigaray Reader*, ed Toril Moi, Blackwell 1991
Alan Jenkins: [review of *The First Earthquake*], *The Observer*, 17 December 1989
Norman Jope: [review of *Dressed As For a Tarot Pack*], *Memes*, 4, 1990
David Kennedy: "Bogus Journeys [review of *Under the Reservoir*]", *The Honest Ulsterman*, no. 94, 88-90
Paul Klee: *Credo*, in *The Inward Vision: Watercolours, Drawings and Writings by Paul Klee*, Abrams, New York 1959, 5
Chris Knight: *Blood Relations: Menstruation and the origins of culture*, Yale University Press, 1992
Julia Kristeva: *The Kristeva Reader*, ed Toril Moi, Blackwell 1986
— *Desire in Language: A Semiotic Approach to Literature and Art*, ed Leon Roudiez, tr Thomas Gora, Alice Jardine & Leon Roudiez, Blackwell 1982
— *Revolution in Poetic Language*, tr Margaret Walker, Columbia University Press, New York 1984
— *Tales of Love*, tr Leon S. Roudiez, Columbia University Press, New York 1987
James Lawler: *Rimbaud's Theatre of the Self*, Harvard University Press, Cambridge, Mass., 1992
D.H. Lawrence: *A Selection From Phoenix*, ed. A.A.H. Inglis, Penguin 1977
Edna Longley: [review of *The First Earthquake*], *London Review of Books*, 22 March 1990
Jean MacVean: [review of *The First Earthquake*], *Temenos*, 11, 1990
Elaine Marks & Isabelle de Courtivron, eds: *New French Feminisms: An Anthology*, Harvester Wheatsheaf 1981
Margaret Marshall: [review of *Dressed As For a Tarot Pack*], *Outposts*, 167, Winter 1990
Sally Munt, ed: *New Lesbian Criticism: Literary and Cultural Readings*, Harvester Wheatsheaf 1992
Shirley Nicholson, ed: *The Goddess Re-Awakening: The Feminine Principle Today*, The Theosophical Publishing House, Wheaton, Illinois 1989

Novalis: *Pollen and Fragments: Selected Poetry and Prose*, tr Arthur Versluis, Phanes Press, Grand Rapids, 1989
—*Works* (Minor), Schlegel, Paris, 1837
—*Novalis Schriften. Die Werke Friedrichs von Hardenberg*, ed Richard Samuel, Hans-Joachim Mähl & Gerhard Schulz, Kohlhammer, Stuttgart 1960-88
Jeff Nutall: [review of *The First Earthquake*], *Time Out*, 8 November 1989
Bernard O'Donoghue: "Drinking it in [review of *Under the Reservoir*]", *Times Literary Supplement*, 1992
G. Pawling: "Alchemy of the Green Man", *Delta*, 58, 1978, 1-10
Michael Payne: *Reading Theory: An Introduction to Lacan, Derrida, and Kristeva*, Blackwell 1993
Pascal Petit: [review of *Under the Reservoir* and *The Laborators*], *Poetry London Newsletter*, IV, vol 3, May 1993, 28
Monique Plaza: ""Phallomorphic power" and the psychology of "woman"", *Ideology and Consciousness*, 4, Autumn 1978
Kathleen Raine: *The Tablet*, 25 November 1989
Jay Ramsay: [review of *The Black Goddess*], *Poetry Review*, 1989/90
Peter Reading: [review of *The First Earthquake*], *The Sunday Times*, 8 October 1989
Rainer Maria Rilke: *Letters on Cézanne*, ed. Clara Rilke, Cape, 1988
—*Duino Elegies*, tr J.B. Leishman & Stephen Spender, Hogarth Press, 1957
Arthur Rimbaud: *Complete Works, Selected Letters*, tr. Wallace Fowlie, University of Chicago Press, Chicago 1966
Neil Roberts: *The Lover, The Dreamer and the World: The Poetry of Peter Redgrove*, Sheffield Academic Press 1994
—"Peter Redgrove: Drinking as Menses-Envy", in S. Vice, T. Armstrong & M. Campbell, eds: *Beyond the Pleasure Dome: Writing and Addiction from the Romantics*, Sheffield Academic Press 1994
Meg Ruth: [review of *The Black Goddess*], *Celtic Dawn*, 3, 1989
Eva Salzman: "A Certain Tang [review of *Under the Reservoir*]", *Poetry Review*, Winter 1992-3, vol 8, no 4, 81
Katon Shual: [review of *The Black Goddess*], *Nuit-Isis*, vol.1, no.6
Penelope Shuttle: *The Orchard Upstairs*, Oxford University Press, 1980
—*The Child-Stealer*, Oxford University Press, 1983
—*The Lion From Rio*, Oxford University Press, 1986
—*Adventures With My Horse*, Oxford University Press, 1988
—*Taxing the Rain*, Oxford University Press, 1992
Anne Stevenson: "Molecules for Eternity", *Poetry Review*, 77, 3, Autumn

1987

Stella Stocker: "Celebration, Love and Lament [review of *Under the Reservoir*]", *Orbis*, 1992, 46-48

Starfire, vol. 1, no.3, Summer 1989

R.J. Stewart: *The Mystic Life of Merlin*, Routledge 1987

Adam Thorpe: *Literary Review*, 1990

Paul Valéry: *An Introduction to the Method of Leonardo da Vinci*, 1894, in *An Anthology,* selected by James Lawler, Routledge 1977

John Powell Ward: [review of *The First Earthquake*], *Poetry Review*, 1989/90

Marina Warner: *London Review of Books*, 6 July 1989

THE ART OF ANDY GOLDSWORTHY

COMPLETE WORKS: SPECIAL EDITION
(PAPERBACK and HARDBACK)

by William Malpas

A new, special edition of the study of the contemporary British sculptor, Andy Goldsworthy, including a new introduction, new bibliography and many new illustrations.

This is the most comprehensive, up-to-date, well-researched and in-depth account of Goldsworthy's art available anywhere.

Andy Goldsworthy makes land art. His sculpture is a sensitive, intuitive response to nature, light, time, growth, the seasons and the earth. Goldsworthy's environmental art is becoming ever more popular: 1993's art book *Stone* was a bestseller; the press raved about Goldsworthy taking over a number of London West End art galleries in 1994; during 1995 Goldsworthy designed a set of Royal Mail stamps and had a show at the British Museum. Malpas surveys all of Goldsworthy's art, and analyzes his relation with other land artists such as Robert Smithson, Walter de Maria, Richard Long and David Nash, and his place in the contemporary British art scene.

The Art of Andy Goldsworthy discusses all of Goldsworthy's important and recent exhibitions and books, including the *Sheepfolds* project; the TV documentaries; *Wood* (1996); the New York Holocaust memorial (2003); and Goldsworthy's collaboration on a dance performance.

Illustrations: 70 b/w, 1 colour. 330 pages. New, special, 2nd edition.
Publisher: Crescent Moon Publishing. Distributor: Gardners Books.

ISBN 1-86171-059-3 (9781861710598) (Paperback) £25.00 / $44.00

ISBN 1-86171-080-1 (9781861710802) (Hardback) £60.00 / $105.00

ANDY GOLDSWORTHY IN CLOSE-UP

SPECIAL EDITION (HARDBACK and PAPERBACK)

by William Malpas

A new, special edition of our bestselling title, exploring Andy Goldsworthy's artworks in detail. A good, all-round introduction to Goldsworthy's art.

Illustrations: 160 b/w, 4 colour. 260 pages. Second edition. Hardback. Publisher: Crescent Moon Publishing. Distributor: Gardners Books.

ISBN 1-86171-094-1 (9781861710949) (Hbk) £60.00 / $105.00

ISBN 1-86171-091-7 (9781861710919) (Pbk) £25.00 / $44.00

Available from bookstores. amazon.com, play.com, tesco.com, and other websites.
In the United States from Baker & Taylor, (800) 7753760 or (800) 7751100 or (908) 5417062. electser@btol.com or btinfo@btol.com.

ANDY GOLDSWORTHY

TOUCHING NATURE:
SPECIAL EDITION

(PAPERBACK and HARDBACK)

by William Malpas

A new, special and updated edition of our bestselling title, providing an excellent general introduction to the art of Andy Goldsworthy.

Illustrations: 75 b/w, 2 colour. 354 pages. Third edition. Paperback.

Publisher: Crescent Moon Publishing. Distributor: Gardners Books.

ISBN 1-86171-056-9 (9781861717) (Paperback) £25.00 / $44.00

ISBN 1-86171-087-9 (9781861710871) (Hardback) £60.00 / $105.00

THE ART OF RICHARD LONG

COMPLETE WORKS : SPECIAL EDITION
(HARDBACK and PAPERBACK)

by William Malpas

A new study of the British artist Richard Long, an important contemporary international artist. The most detailed, in-depth exploration of Richard Long's art currently available.

Illustrations: 48 b/w, 2 colour. 439 pages.
First edition. Hardback and paperback editions.

Publisher: Crescent Moon Publishing. Distributor: Gardners Books.

ISBN 1-86171-079-8 (9781861710796) (Hardback) £60.00 / $105.00

ISBN 1-86171-081-X (9781861710819) (Paperback) £25.00 / $44.00

LAND ART

A COMPLETE GUIDE TO LANDSCAPE, ENVIRONMENTAL, EARTHWORKS, NATURE, SCULPTURE AND INSTALLATION ART

by William Malpas

A new, special edition of our popular book on land art.
Chapters on land artists such as Robert Smithson, Walter de Maria, Christo, Michael Heizer, Richard Long and Andy Goldsworthy.

Illustrations: 35 b/w, 2 colour. 314 pages. First edition. Paperback.

Publisher: Crescent Moon Publishing. Distributor: Gardners Books.

ISBN 1-86171-062-3 (9781861710628) £25.00 / $44.00

J.R.R. Tolkien
The Books, The Films, The Whole Cultural Phenomenon

by Jeremy Mark Robinson

A new critical study of J.R.R. Tolkien, creator of Middle-earth and author of *The Lord of the Rings, The Hobbit* and *The Silmarillion*, among other books.

This new critical study explores Tolkien's major writings (*The Lord of the Rings, The Hobbit, Beowulf: The Monster and the Critics, The Letters, The Silmarillion* and *The History of Middle-earth* volumes); Tolkien and fairy tales; the mythological, political and religious aspects of Tolkien's Middle-earth; the critics' response to Tolkien's fiction over the decades; the Tolkien industry (merchandizing, toys, role-playing games, posters, Tolkien societies, conferences and the like); Tolkien in visual and fantasy art; the cultural aspects of The Lord of the Rings (from the 1950s to the present); Tolkien's fiction's relationship with other fantasy fiction, such as C.S. Lewis and *Harry Potter*; and the TV, radio and film versions of Tolkien's books, including the 2001-03 Hollywood interpretations of *The Lord of the Rings*.

This new book draws on contemporary cultural theory and analysis and offers a sympathetic and illuminating (and sceptical) account of the Tolkien phenomenon. This book is designed to appeal to the general reader (and viewer) of Tolkien: it is written in a clear, jargon-free and easily-accessible style.

754pp   ISBN 1-86171-057-7   £25.00 / $37.50

Walerian Borowczyk

Cinema of Erotic Dreams

by Jeremy Mark Robinson

Walerian Borowczyk (1923-2006) was a Polish artist, animator and filmmaker who lived in France for much of his life. He is the author of European art cinema masterpieces Goto: Island of Love, Blanche and Immoral Tales, some surreal animated shorts, and controversial films such as The Beast. This new book concentrates on Borowczyk's feature films, from Goto to Love Rites, which contain some of the most extraordinary images and scenes in recent cinema. Erotica for some, porn for others, Borowczyk's films are highly idiosyncratic and unforgettable.

Bibliography, notes, illustrations 240pp.
Paperback   ISBN 9781861712301   £15.00 / $30.00

Jean-Luc Godard

The Passion of Cinema / Le Passion de Cinéma

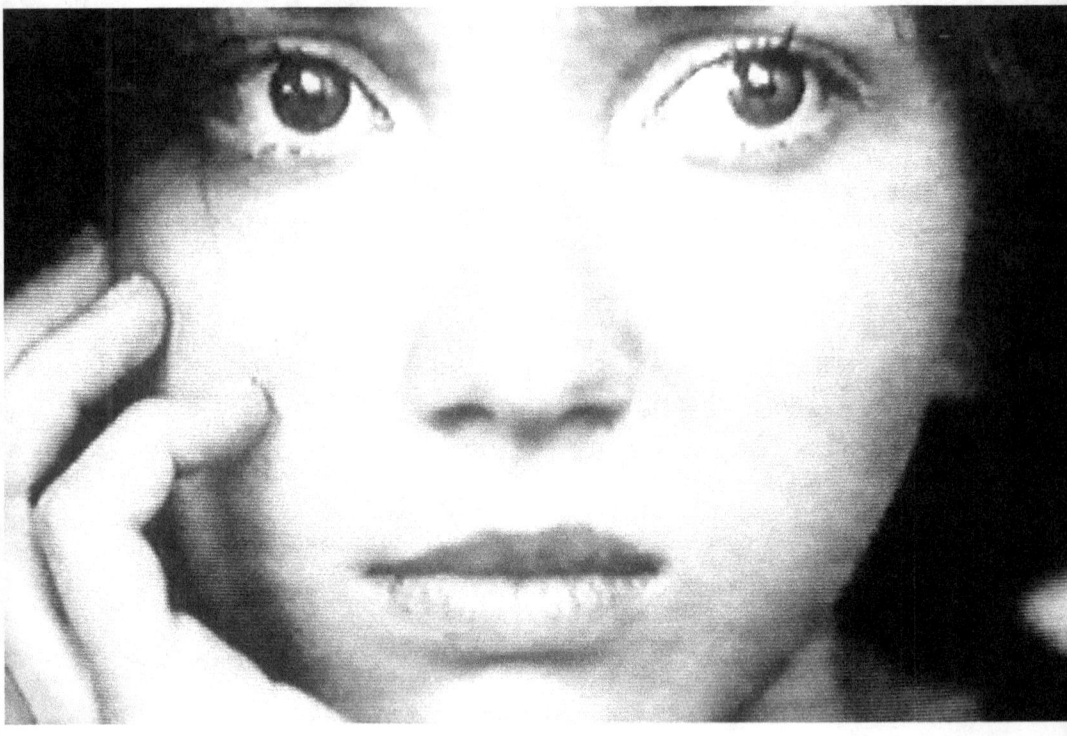

by Jeremy Mark Robinson

A new study of the French filmmaker Jean-Luc Godard (b. 1930), director of iconic films such as *Breathless, Weekend, Pierrot le Fou, Passion* and *Vivre Sa vie*. This book explores 27 of Godard's major films, from *Breathless* to *Notre Musique*, and includes a scene by scene analysis of Godard's controversial 1985 movie of the Virgin Mary, *Je Vous Salue, Marie*.

Bibliography, notes, illustrations   420pp
Hardback   ISBN 9781761712271   £50.00 / $100.00

THE SACRED CINEMA OF ANDREI TARKOVSKY

by Jeremy Mark Robinson

A new study of the Russian filmmaker Andrei Tarkovsky (1932-1986), director of seven feature films, including *Andrei Roublyov, Mirror, Solaris, Stalker* and *The Sacrifice*.
This is one of the most comprehensive and detailed studies of Tarkovsky's cinema available. Every film is explored in depth, with scene-by-scene analyses. All aspects of Tarkovsky's output are critiqued, including editing, camera, staging, script, budget, collaborations, production, sound, music, performance and spirituality. Tarkovsky is placed with a European New Wave tradition of filmmaking, alongside directors like Ingmar Bergman, Carl Theodor Dreyer, Pier Paolo Pasolini and Robert Bresson.
An essential addition to film studies.

Illustrations: 150 b/w, 4 colour. 682 pages. First edition. Hardback.

Publisher: Crescent Moon Publishing. Distributor: Gardners Books.

ISBN 1-86171-096-8 (9781861710963) £60.00 / $105.00

Life, Life
Selected Poems

Arseny Tarkovsky

translated and edited by Virginia Rounding

Arseny Tarkovsky is the neglected Russian poet, father of the acclaimed film director Andrei Tarkovsky. This new book gathers together many of Tarkovsky's most lyrical and heartfelt poems, in Rounding's clear, new translations. Many of Tarkovsky's poems appeared in his son's films, such as *Mirror, Stalker, Nostalghia* and *The Sacrifice*.
There is an introduction by Rounding, and a bibliography of both Arseny and Andrei Tarkovsky.

Bibliography and notes   110pp   2nd ed   ISBN 1-86171-114-X   £10.00 / $20.00

In the Dim Void

Samuel Beckett's Late Trilogy: *Company, Ill Seen, Ill Said* and *Worstward Ho*

by Gregory Johns

This book discusses the luminous beauty and dense, rigorous poetry of Beckett's late works, *Company, Ill Seen, Ill Said* and *Worstward Ho*. Johns looks back over Beckett's long writing career, charting the development from the *Molloy-Malone Dies-Unnamable* trilogy through the 'fizzles' of the 1960s to the elegiac lyricism of the *Company* series. Johns compares the trilogy with late plays such as *Ghosts, Footfalls* and *Rockaby*.

Bibliography, notes. 120pp
ISBN 1861710712 and ISBN 1861712356   £10.00 / $20.00

CRESCENT MOON PUBLISHING

ARTS, PAINTING, SCULPTURE

The Art of Andy Goldsworthy: Complete Works
Andy Goldsworthy: Touching Nature
Andy Goldsworthy in Close-Up
Andy Goldsworthy: Pocket Guide
Andy Goldsworthy In America
Land Art: A Complete Guide
Richard Long: The Art of Walking
The Art of Richard Long: Complete Works
Richard Long in Close-Up
Richard Long: Pocket Guide
Land Art In the UK
Land Art in Close-Up
Land Art In the U.S.A.
Land Art: Pocket Guide
Installation Art in Close-Up
Minimal Art and Artists In the 1960s and After
Colourfield Painting
Land Art DVD, TV documentary
Andy Goldsworthy DVD, TV documentary
The Erotic Object: Sexuality in Sculpture From Prehistory to the Present Day
Sex in Art: Pornography and Pleasure in Painting and Sculpture
Postwar Art
Sacred Gardens: The Garden in Myth, Religion and Art
Glorification: Religious Abstraction in Renaissance and 20th Century Art
Early Netherlandish Painting
Leonardo da Vinci
Piero della Francesca
Giovanni Bellini
Fra Angelico: Art and Religion in the Renaissance
Mark Rothko: The Art of Transcendence
Frank Stella: American Abstract Artist
Jasper Johns: Painting By Numbers
Brice Marden
Alison Wilding: The Embrace of Sculpture
Vincent van Gogh: Visionary Landscapes
Eric Gill: Nuptials of God
Constantin Brancusi: Sculpting the Essence of Things
Max Beckmann
Caravaggio
Gustave Moreau
Egon Schiele: Sex and Death In Purple Stockings
Delizioso Fotografico Fervore: Works In Process 1
Sacro Cuore: Works In Process 2
The Light Eternal: J.M.W. Turner
The Madonna Glorified: Karen Arthurs

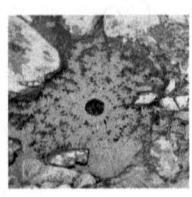

LITERATURE

J.R.R. Tolkien: The Books, The Films, The Whole Cultural Phenomenon
J.R.R. Tolkien: Pocket Guide
Tolkien's Heroic Quest
The *Earthsea* Books of Ursula Le Guin
Beauties, Beasts and Enchantment: Classic French Fairy Tales
Sexing Hardy: Thomas Hardy and Feminism
Thomas Hardy's *Tess of the d'Urbervilles*
Thomas Hardy's *Jude the Obscure*
Thomas Hardy: The Tragic Novels
Love and Tragedy: Thomas Hardy
The Poetry of Landscape in Hardy
Wessex Revisited: Thomas Hardy and John Cowper Powys
Wolfgang Iser: Essays and Interviews
Petrarch, Dante and the Troubadours
Maurice Sendak and the Art of Children's Book Illustration
Andrea Dworkin
Cixous, Irigaray, Kristeva: The *Jouissance* of French Feminism
Julia Kristeva: Art, Love, Melancholy, Philosophy, Semiotics and Psychoanalysis
Hélene Cixous I Love You: The *Jouissance* of Writing
Luce Irigaray: Lips, Kissing, and the Politics of Sexual Difference
Peter Redgrove: Here Comes the Flood
Peter Redgrove: Sex-Magic-Poetry-Cornwall
Lawrence Durrell: Between Love and Death, East and West
Love, Culture & Poetry: Lawrence Durrell
Cavafy: Anatomy of a Soul
German Romantic Poetry: Goethe, Novalis, Heine, Hölderlin
Feminism and Shakespeare
Shakespeare: Love, Poetry & Magic
The Passion of D.H. Lawrence
D.H. Lawrence: Symbolic Landscapes
D.H. Lawrence: Infinite Sensual Violence
Rimbaud: Arthur Rimbaud and the Magic of Poetry
The Ecstasies of John Cowper Powys
Sensualism and Mythology: The Wessex Novels of John Cowper Powys
Amorous Life: John Cowper Powys and the Manifestation of Affectivity (H.W. Fawkner)
Postmodern Powys: New Essays on John Cowper Powys (Joe Boulter)
Rethinking Powys: Critical Essays on John Cowper Powys
Paul Bowles & Bernardo Bertolucci
Rainer Maria Rilke
Joseph Conrad: *Heart of Darkness*
In the Dim Void: Samuel Beckett
Samuel Beckett Goes into the Silence
André Gide: Fiction and Fervour
Jackie Collins and the Blockbuster Novel
Blinded By Her Light: The Love-Poetry of Robert Graves
The Passion of Colours: Travels In Mediterranean Lands
Poetic Forms

POETRY

Ursula Le Guin: Walking In Cornwall
Peter Redgrove: Here Comes The Flood
Peter Redgrove: Sex-Magic-Poetry-Cornwall
Dante: Selections From the *Vita Nuova*
Petrarch, Dante and the Troubadours
William Shakespeare: *The Sonnets*
William Shakespeare: Complete Poems
Blinded By Her Light: The Love-Poetry of Robert Graves
Emily Dickinson: Selected Poems
Emily Brontë: Poems
Thomas Hardy: Selected Poems
Percy Bysshe Shelley: Poems
John Keats: Selected Poems
D.H. Lawrence: Selected Poems
Edmund Spenser: Poems
Edmund Spenser: *Amoretti*
John Donne: Poems
Henry Vaughan: Poems
Sir Thomas Wyatt: Poems
Robert Herrick: Selected Poems
Rilke: Space, Essence and Angels in the Poetry of Rainer Maria Rilke
Rainer Maria Rilke: Selected Poems
Friedrich Hölderlin: Selected Poems
Arseny Tarkovsky: Selected Poems
Novalis: *Hymns To the Night*
Paul Verlaine: Selected Poems
Arthur Rimbaud: Selected Poems
Arthur Rimbaud: *A Season in Hell*
Arthur Rimbaud and the Magic of Poetry
D.J. Enright: By-Blows
Jeremy Reed: Brigitte's Blue Heart
Jeremy Reed: Claudia Schiffer's Red Shoes
Gorgeous Little Orpheus
Radiance: New Poems
Crescent Moon Book of Nature Poetry
Crescent Moon Book of Love Poetry
Crescent Moon Book of Mystical Poetry
Crescent Moon Book of Elizabethan Love Poetry
Crescent Moon Book of Metaphysical Poetry
Crescent Moon Book of Romantic Poetry
Pagan America: New American Poetry

MEDIA, CINEMA, FEMINISM and CULTURAL STUDIES

J.R.R. Tolkien: The Books, The Films, The Whole Cultural Phenomenon
J.R.R. Tolkien: Pocket Guide
The *Lord of the Rings* Movies: Pocket Guide
The Ghost Dance: The Origins of Religion
Cixous, Irigaray, Kristeva: The *Jouissance* of French Feminism
Julia Kristeva: Art, Love, Melancholy, Philosophy, Semiotics and Psychoanalysis
Luce Irigaray: Lips, Kissing, and the Politics of Sexual Difference
Hélene Cixous I Love You: The *Jouissance* of Writing
Andrea Dworkin
'Cosmo Woman': The World of Women's Magazines
Women in Pop Music
Discovering the Goddess (Geoffrey Ashe)
The Poetry of Cinema
The Sacred Cinema of Andrei Tarkovsky
Andrei Tarkovsky: Pocket Guide
Andrei Tarkovsky: *Mirror*: Pocket Movie Guide
Andrei Tarkovsky: *The Sacrifice*: Pocket Movie Guide
Walerian Borowczyk: Cinema of Erotic Dreams
Jean-Luc Godard: The Passion of Cinema
John Hughes and Eighties Cinema
Ferris Bueller's Day Off: Pocket Movie Guide
Jean-Luc Godard: Pocket Guide
The Cinema of Richard Linklater
Liv Tyler: Star In Ascendance
Blade Runner and the Films of Philip K. Dick
Paul Bowles and Bernardo Bertolucci
Media Hell: Radio, TV and the Press
An Open Letter to the BBC
Detonation Britain: Nuclear War in the UK
Feminism and Shakespeare
Wild Zones: Pornography, Art and Feminism
Sex in Art: Pornography and Pleasure in Painting and Sculpture
Sexing Hardy: Thomas Hardy and Feminism

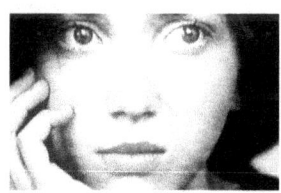

In my view *The Light Eternal* is among the very best of all the material I read on Turner. (Douglas Graham, director of the Turner Museum, Denver, Colorado)

The Light Eternal is a model monograph, an exemplary job. The subject matter of the book is beautifully organised and dead on beam. (Lawrence Durrell)

It is amazing for me to see my work treated with such passion and respect. (Andrea Dworkin)

Sex-Magic-Poetry-Cornwall is a very rich essay... It is like a brightly-lighted box. (Peter Redgrove)

CRESCENT MOON PUBLISHING

www.ingramcontent.com/pod-product-compliance
Lightning Source LLC
Chambersburg PA
CBHW062205080426

42734CB00010B/1792